The zen environment is something that has to be experienced directly with the whole body and mind, and all I can do is try, in this book, to show you a way to experience it yourself. But I might just point to the calligraphy Katagiri Roshi painted especially for this book. He chose the characters that mean "the sound of falling in drops" and explained his choice this way:

> Zen environments lie nowhere but in our everyday living, existing just like the process of falling in drops. How do we listen to the sound of falling in drops? By leaving no space between ourselves, as listeners, and each drop. And by not clinging to any special drop. At this very moment can you be alive to this sound? Can you be aware of the process of your own life falling in drops—without freezing a drop of it?

—Marian Mountain in the Prologue
to *The Zen Environment*

BANTAM NEW AGE BOOKS

This important new imprint—to include books in a variety of fields and disciplines—will deal with the search for meaning, growth and change. BANTAM NEW AGE BOOKS will form connecting patterns to help understand this search as well as mankind's options and models for tomorrow. They are books that circumscribe our times and our future.

LIFETIDE by Lyall Watson
THE LIVES OF A CELL by Lewis Thomas
LOST CHRISTIANITY by Jacob Needleman
MAGICAL CHILD by Joseph Chilton Pearce
THE MEDUSA AND THE SNAIL by Lewis Thomas
MIND AND NATURE by Gregory Bateson
MIRROR, MASK, AND SHADOW by Sheldon Kopp
MYSTICISM AND THE NEW PHYSICS by Michael Talbot
NEW RULES by Daniel Yankelovich
THE RED LIMIT by Timothy Ferris
THE SCIENTIST by John C. Lilly, M.D.
THE SILENT PULSE by George Leonard
STALKING THE WILD PENDULUM by Itzhak Bentov
STRESS AND THE ART OF BIOFEEDBACK by Barbara B. Brown
THE TAO OF PHYSICS by Fritjof Capra
TO HAVE OR TO BE? by Erich Fromm
THE TURNING POINT by Fritjof Capra
VOLUNTARY SIMPLICITY by Duane Elgin
THE WAY OF THE SHAMAN: A GUIDE TO POWER AND
    HEALING by Michael Harner
THE WINE OF LIFE AND OTHER ESSAYS by Harold Morowitz
ZEN AND THE ART OF MOTORCYCLE MAINTENANCE
    by Robert H. Pirsig
THE ZEN ENVIRONMENT by Marian Mountain

滴滴聲

THE ZEN ENVIRONMENT

The Impact of Zen Meditation

Marian Mountain

With an Introduction by
Dainin Katagiri Roshi

And a Foreword by
Robert M. Pirsig

BANTAM BOOKS
TORONTO · NEW YORK · LONDON · SYDNEY

This low-priced Bantam Book
has been completely reset in a type face
designed for easy reading, and was printed
from new plates. It contains the complete
text of the original hard-cover edition.
NOT ONE WORD HAS BEEN OMITTED.

THE ZEN ENVIRONMENT:
THE IMPACT OF ZEN MEDITATION

A Bantam Book / published by arrangement with
William Morrow and Company, Inc.

PRINTING HISTORY
William Morrow edition published February 1982
Bantam edition / April 1983

New Age and the accompanying figure design as well as the
statement "a search for meaning, growth and change" are
trademarks of Bantam Books, Inc.

ISBN 0-553-23060-3

Published simultaneously in the United States and Canada

Bantam Books are published by Bantam Books, Inc. Its trade-
mark, consisting of the words "Bantam Books" and the por-
trayal of a rooster, is registered in U.S. Patent and Trademark
Office and in other countries. Marca Registrada. Bantam
Books, Inc., 666 Fifth Avenue, New York, New York 10103.

To my zen master,
Shunryu Suzuki Roshi

Even to share the shade of one tree, or to draw water from the same river is due to one's past *karma;* how much more so in our case!

—*The Old Woman of the Mountains*
A Japanese *Noh* play

Foreword

Zen literature seems at times to divide into two groups of works: those that are *about* zen; and those that *are* zen itself, talking. The first group is often precise, authoritative, and highly pedigreed but lacks a certain warmth and settledness. The second is often inaccurate, poorly composed, vague at times but has a special sound which you can recognize as the real thing. It is the sound of someone singing a song he himself has composed and which no one else can ever quite imitate. That is what we have here.

Zen is nothing other than what happens to individual people, and zen accounts which stay close to personal circumstances are truer than those which generalize. When Marian keeps her accounting close to what she sees and remembers, she avoids the academic objectification of zen which becomes controversial and misleading.

My own academic, English teacher's narrow mind always bridles at rambling zen disquisitions of this sort, but if you want to read real zen you have to put up with it. The best of zen masters ramble on and on without any apparent central point. This is caused by the slippery nature of what they are trying to convey. You can't read a zen discourse the way you read a detective story, trying to figure out the plot. There isn't any. You have to read this book like a giant catalog, line by line, looking for items to buy and keeping the rest on hand in case you might want to buy them later. When you finish this book, you can start right in again on the first chapter and discover much more than you saw the first time.

That, after all, is how one learns about life itself.

—ROBERT M. PIRSIG

Contents

PART TWO
SETTLING DOWN IN THE ZEN ENVIRONMENT

PART THREE
CULTIVATING THE ZEN ENVIRONMENT

Introduction

I want to introduce you to Marian Mountain, author of this book. I have followed Marian's zen career since the early 1960s when she first began to practice meditation under the guidance of the late Shunryu Suzuki Roshi. Marian never considered zen just as a principle or philosophy of life. Her enthusiastic zen spirit, which was motivated by a strong desire to free herself and others from suffering, expressed itself in all aspects of her daily living.

The explanation of zen in this book is as clear as spring water that oozes from the depths of mountains. It is sure to satisfy anyone who is interested in improving the quality of human life. When I read this book, it reminded me of a zen story about a famous zen master called Joshu:

One day, when he was practicing zen in the monastery under his master, Nansen, Joshu shut the kitchen door and stirred up the fire until volumes of smoke filled the room. Then Joshu shouted, "Fire! Fire! Put it out!" When all the monks and the zen master hurried to the kitchen to help put out the fire, Joshu refused to open the door. Instead he said nonchalantly, "If anyone can give me a word that will turn my delusion into enlightenment, I will open the door." Everyone was speechless. Except Nansen who silently handed Joshu a key through the kitchen window. With this key Joshu opened the door.

In this story Joshu and his master show us, by dramatic means, the whole problem of human suffering—what causes it and how to escape from it. Most people act just like Joshu. They close the door and stir up the fire. They close their minds and stir up their desires. On the surface they may appear to be enjoying their lives, but inside they are suffering from the delusions that fill their minds.

Many people are attracted to zen because they think it may help them get rid of their suffering. They expect to have their delusion turned into enlightenment just by hearing some enlightening words from a zen master. But at the same time they stubbornly refuse to open their minds. What can a zen master do when he encounters such people? It is impossible to help them by any kind of philosophical, psychological, ethical, or logical discussion. To help them a zen master must be able to take advantage of any opportunity to throw a key quickly into their minds.

Zen masters use vivid methods to save people from their delusions. Sometimes they shout at their students; sometimes they give them blows. Why is this kind of lively activity so very important in zen? Because it is the real living way to throw a key to someone who is suffering.

This book is like a key to throw into your mind. This key can open your mind. But only if you *use* it. It depends on you, whether you choose to use this key to free yourself, or not. So after you finish reading this book, I encourage you to follow the suggestions in it. Then you will be able to experience for yourself the satisfaction of living your own life in the vivid reality of the zen environment.

—DAININ KATAGIRI ROSHI (Zen Master)
Minnesota Zen Meditation Center
Minneapolis, Minnesota

Prologue

*T*he *Zen Environment* is an attempt to present an ecological zen experience, to integrate zen philosophy, zen practice, and zen life. Strictly speaking, this is impossible to do in words. But I had to try it anyway. Even if I failed. Failure is a good zen teacher. If someone were to ask me today, "What is zen?" I'd say, "Zen is the art of failure." There were times when I was writing this book that I thought I'd call it *Zen and the Art of Failure*.

Which brings me to a warning: Readers unfamiliar with zen meditation and zen life should be careful not to jump to the conclusion that the zen environment explored in this book is a representative one. Even though the practice of zen meditation may be the same for everyone, the impact is always unique. There can be no such thing as a typical zen environment, or a typical zen master, or a typical zen student. The practice of zen, which is not only a unique form of sitting meditation but also an attitude that affects every aspect of the zen student's life, is what makes me uniquely me, and you uniquely you. It is what reveals our true identity.

Neither should readers expect to react to *The Zen Environment* in the same manner as the zen masters who wrote the introduction to it. Just because Katagiri Roshi found satisfaction in reading this book doesn't necessarily mean that you will. In fact, there may be many sections of the book that you will find disturbing. The impact of zen meditation on a good zen student is like the impact of a river upon a salmon fighting its way upstream to spawn. A zen master, having made this journey upstream many times, feels at home in the river. No matter where he finds himself in the river, he always realizes his direct connection with the source. The ordinary person has lost this connection. As you can probably see, there is a big difference in the impact of the river, depending on whether you are flowing *with* it like a baby salmon or *against* it like a mature salmon.

So, to the zen student, the first journey up the stream of zen life is usually a rough one. There are many obstacles in the way: rapids, waterfalls, narrows, nets, and hooks. And beautiful calm pools that invite the weary traveler to give up the struggle and just settle down under some big rock. But there is no settling down in the zen environment—not even after reaching the source.

At this point you probably would like me to clarify for you, in a few words, what the zen environment is. I don't think I can. The zen environment is something that has to be experienced directly with the whole body and mind, and all I can do is try, in this book, to show you a way to experience it yourself. But if it were absolutely necessary that I define the zen environment right now, in a few words, I might just point to the calligraphy Katagiri Roshi painted especially for this book. He chose the characters that mean "the sound of falling in drops" and explained his choice this way:

Zen environments lie nowhere but in our everyday living, existing just like the process of falling in drops. How do we listen to the sound of falling in drops? By leaving no space between ourselves, as listeners, and each drop. And by not clinging to any special drop. At this very moment can you be alive to this sound? Can you be aware of the process of your own life falling in drops—without freezing a drop of it?

One of the greatest problems in writing or reading a book on zen is the danger of freezing the flow of zen life into a solid block that cuts off movement in all directions.

But if there are no gaps between the reader and the writer, and there is no clinging or resistance to any of the words, then there is a possibility that a book on zen can remain fluid, and its impact can be a freeing, rather than a freezing, experience.

PART ONE

Exploring
the
Zen
Environment

Note

Please refer to the glossary for definitions of foreign words and Buddhist technical terms, as well as details about historical persons and places mentioned in the text. To make reading easier, diacritical marks on foreign words have been restricted to the glossary. Sources of quotations can be found in the notes section.

I

My Old Hometown

We're on the road again. Living in our only permanent home, a tiny trailer I call Samsara (Wanderer). Sometimes we are amazed that two people can live in such a small space. But space, as well as time, is relative. Meditation, as the Indian lay Buddhist philosopher Vimalakirti demonstrated, can expand even a ten-foot-square room into infinite proportions.

Today we may make our home in this Pacific valley, sheltered from the shifting winds of fortune, but tomorrow we may be blown along like a cloud in the sky, or whirled about like a bubble in a stream. So we might as well enjoy this place now. It's all we have.

We've been here before. And yet this is the first time we've been here. Since everything is changing, everything is always fresh and new. This is the beginning of a new zen day. The dew sparkles on each leaf and every blade of grass. It is quiet and peaceful here. The campground is spacious, and since it is off-season we have the place almost to ourselves. The noise of the traffic on the Coast Highway is muffled by a screen of tall cypress trees. From our campsite we can't see the ocean. But it's not far away. Later on we'll walk down to the beach. We may leave a few footprints in the sand for the incoming tide to wash away.

We drink our second cup of coffee outside, sitting at the picnic table under a tree blooming with yellow flowers. The sun rises over the mountain behind us, warming the air. A few orange and black butterflies begin to stir. Within an hour, hundreds of them are fluttering around the tree, feeding on the yellow blossoms, resting on the green leaves, and coupling on the edges of our empty coffee cups.

Once I dreamt that I was a butterfly called Emptiness. Now I dream that I am a woman called Marian. In this dream I am married to a man called Jack. We live in a fantasy called Big Sur; it's part of an imaginary state called California that exists for a moment in a vision called America, on an illusion called Earth, in a science fiction plot called the Solar System, in a beautiful theory called the Milky Way, and floats in a zen environment called Vast Emptiness.

In this dream Jack and I call ourselves Big Sur caretakers. Since caretaking positions don't always provide a house to live in, we find it convenient to take our home with us like hermit crabs. Caretaking seldom provides an income either, so we find it necessary to pick up odd jobs to fill the tank of our truck and stock the shelves of our trailer. My traveling companion in this life is a Jack-of-all-trades. I am a master of none. At the present moment we are between caretaking jobs, waiting for an opening. Big Sur is a beautiful environment, so there are always more caretakers than places to take care of here. But over the years we've learned to be very patient. Sooner or later we always seem to find the right spot.

A flash of vermilion in the sky sends Jack running to the truck for his binoculars. It's a hang glider. Or is it a butterfly? It doesn't really matter what it is called. Since it is floating into our dream space, it is ours for this moment to enjoy.

Behind the campground there is a dirt road that winds up the mountain to a flat, high above the ocean. Here the butterfly-men hurl themselves into emptiness. For a while they realize themselves, and help us realize too, that we are all supported and transported in this dream of life by nothing but emptiness.

Jack hands me the binoculars. Now I can see the young man hanging below his vermilion sail. He looks relaxed. He shifts the weight of his body occasionally so that the craft circles in large spirals, some of them taking him over the ocean. As he nears the ground his circles become smaller. Now he has dropped out of sight behind the cypress trees. He will land on a large field above the beach. After he touches the ground he will run a few feet and then walk across the field to where his friends are waiting for him. His journey of solitude and silence has lasted only twenty minutes, but its effects will linger for several days.

Each of us has our favorite form of meditation. Some meditate when they play golf, some when they jog or ski. I know a man who meditates when he builds rock walls, and a woman who meditates when she sews. Jack meditates whenever he gets under the hood of his truck. Zen masters meditate when they sit, or stand, or walk, or lie down, or eat, or go to the bathroom. Some people have never forgotten how to meditate. Others have to be taught, or reminded, how to meditate. Without some form of meditation this dream called life becomes a nightmare. Meditation reconnects us with the zen environment which the first zen patriach, Bodhidharma, called Vast Emptiness.

Jack asks me if I would like to walk down to the field with him to the place where the hang-glider families are gathered around their bright-colored sails. I have some letters to write, so I resist the tempting invitation. There is one letter in particular that I have been putting off writing. I *should* write to my mother. In her last letter to me she asked me this question: "When are you going to settle down?"

This isn't an easy question to answer. I thought of writing my mother that living in Samsara is like living in *nirvana*. But then I would have had to write a book to try to explain to my mother what I meant.

Samsara is the wandering life; *samsara* is the wandering mind. Wandering is the Buddhist way of expressing our ordinary life and our ordinary mind. *Nirvana*—well, strictly speaking, it is the same as *samsara*. Before enlightenment, we are convinced that *nirvana* is the opposite of *samsara*. After enlightenment we realize *nirvana* is the same as *samsara*, and enlightened life is the same as ordinary life.

Maybe it would help to clarify the seeming difference (but actual identity) of the states of *nirvana* and *samsara* (the enlightened life-mind and the ordinary life-mind) if we consider another Buddhist term that is sometimes used as a synonym for *nirvana* but can also be used as a synonym for *samsara*. The Sanskrit word *apratistha* literally means, according to the late Zen Buddhist scholar, D. T. Suzuki, "not to have any home where one may settle down." Actually, D. T. Suzuki says that *apratistha* means "to settle down where there is no settling down." Not to have any home where one may settle down—that may seem terrible. But to settle down where there is no settling down—that may be wonderful.

Samsara and *nirvana*. They are almost the same, but not exactly. D. T. Suzuki translated a verse from a Japanese book of swordsmanship which expresses this attitude better than I could in words:

> *Wherever and whenever the mind is found*
>   *attached to anything*
> *Make haste to detach yourself from it.*
> *When you tarry for any length of time*
> *It will turn again into your old hometown.*

It is important to remember that mind, in Zen Buddhism, is not separate from, or dependent upon, the body or the total environment. Our old hometown is not just a place. It is also a state of mind, our egoistic description of reality, which limits our awareness by tethering it to words, concepts, and reasons.

The great zen patriarch Rinzai described the spirit of *apratistha* as the Man of No Title, who, he said, "is the one who is in the house and yet does not stay away from the road; he is the one who is on the road and yet does not stay away from the house. Is he an ordinary man or a great sage? No one can tell. Even the Devil does not know where to locate him. Even the Buddha fails to manage him as he may desire. When we try to point him out, he is no more there; he is on the other side of the mountain."

It might be easier for my mother to accept my unsettled life-style if I were a young woman. But I'm not. I'm middle-aged, with grown children of my own. Before I took up the practice of zen I *was* settled down (or so I thought), living in a pleasant middle-class neighborhood in a small suburban town near San Francisco. I was divorced. I had a part-time career. I owned a comfortable home, had a good income, plenty of freedom, good health, intelligent children, and interesting friends. But for some unknown reason I felt dissatisfied. I had the feeling that something was missing from my life.

I began searching for the cause of my unreasonable dissatisfaction. It was during this search that I signed up for a weekend seminar on meditation at Esalen Institute in Big Sur. Esalen is often described as the home of the human-potential movement. But for me Esalen will always be the home of Buddhism. Esalen is a place where trees and people miraculously flower out of season. It was at Esalen (or was it at the Lumbini Gardens where Buddha was born?) that the Zen Buddhist poet Gary Snyder taught me how to practice *zazen* (sitting meditation). It was there I got my first taste of zen. I've tried over and over, and failed again and again, to describe the impact of that first zen experience. One of these days I'll go back to Esalen and then I may be able to recapture some of the spirit of that original experience.

Meanwhile, back in my old hometown I began dreaming of going to Japan (after my children were grown) where I would find my own zen master—someone who would liberate me. Every morning I practiced *zazen* so that I'd be prepared for the appearance of my zen master. (I had read somewhere that when the zen student is ready, the zen master will appear.)

Three months later I was drinking a second cup of coffee and skimming through the morning paper when a word jumped off the religious page. I stopped and read the short announcement:

ZEN CLASS TO BEGIN

Next Thursday morning at 5:45 a.m. the Reverend Shunryu Suzuki Roshi, head priest of Sokoji Zen Buddhist Temple in San Francisco, will start a weekly class in zen meditation.

The address was in Palo Alto, just a short drive from my Los Altos home. I was amazed. I had no idea that there was a Japanese zen master with a temple in San

Francisco. Why had no one at the Esalen seminar told me about Suzuki Roshi? Maybe they assumed I knew about him. Maybe I wasn't ready to meet my zen master then. Was I ready now?

Thursday morning. A tree-lined street in Palo Alto. A yellow porch light on one of the old two-story houses was the only sign of life. I found a note thumbtacked to the front door.

THE DOOR IS OPEN. PLEASE COME IN.

In the dim light of the hall I could see a pile of coats and bags on a long bench. There was a row of shoes on the floor. After taking off my coat and shoes, I stepped through the French doors into the living room. I smelled incense. Pine. There were eight or ten people sitting on black cushions in the middle of the room. I spotted an empty cushion, sat down on it, crossed my legs (or more specifically my ankles as my legs were still too stiff to twist into a half-lotus position), and began staring at the pattern in the oriental rug. I head the rustle of silk robes. Someone was standing behind me. . . .

Suzuki Roshi did nothing more than straighten my back and arrange my hands in the right position for *zazen*. Still, I felt something in his total attention that first zen morning that carried me back beyond my earliest recollection. What was it? Love? Great compassion? Then I realized. It was total acceptance. I was a stranger, a new student, awkward and ignorant. Yet I felt that Suzuki Roshi had accepted me as wholeheartedly and uncritically as a mother accepts her newborn child.

After *zazen* Suzuki Roshi led a simplified version of the service he had developed for his American congregation at Zen Center in San Francisco. Then he lectured informally and answered questions. While he was talking I had a chance to observe his appearance and manner. Like many Japanese men Roshi was short and small-boned. He was sixty-one at that time, but his face was smooth and almost unlined. If his head hadn't been shaved he might have appeared to be no older than fifty. Roshi had lively brown eyes and a perky nose. His voice was soft and his laugh a delightful chuckle. All of his movements were as graceful and as unself-conscious as a cat's. I knew I had found my first zen master.

It is traditional in zen training to have three zen masters. Each one represents one phase, more or less, of zen growth. This isn't a rigid rule. Sometimes, as in the case of Suzuki Roshi's successor Zentatsu Baker Roshi, one zen master sees a zen student through all three phases of zen development. There are more than three phases, but I don't intend to talk about the advanced stages of traditional Zen Buddhism in this book.

The first zen master may be likened to a spiritual parent who encourages the student to leave his "old hometown" (his rigid way of viewing life). The relationship of Buddha to his disciples, the relationship of a parent to a child, is a good example of the ideal first phase of zen. The relationship between Suzuki Roshi and myself followed the classic pattern.

One morning after meditation class I invited Suzuki Roshi to come to my home for breakfast before driving him back to his temple in San Francisco. As soon as he walked into the entrance hall of my home he stopped. "Oh, what a bee-oo-tiful *big* living room," he sighed. Though the thought had never entered my mind until that moment, I knew immediately what was in Roshi's mind. He was picturing the room as a *zendo* (meditation room). As we stood at the entrance of the imaginary *zendo*, I began to visualize the black cushions arranged on the grass-green carpet of the room. I could picture Roshi sitting at the end of the room, his brown silk robes set off by the white walls. I could see a Japanese flower arrangement in the alcove above Roshi's head, a fire flickering in the fireplace on cold mornings. . . .

But then my vision was interrupted. I remembered the racket my five teen-age children made getting ready for school. I told Roshi it would never work.

During breakfast Roshi explained to me that he wanted to expand the activities of the zen group. He told me he wasn't worried about my children disturbing the zen students. "Learning to accept the normal noises of one's environment is very good practice for zen students," he said. I thought this over a moment and gave him my answer: "OK. Let's give it a try."

I was hooked. Though nothing formal was ever said, that was the point where I moved from being one of Suzuki Roshi's followers to being one of his disciples. For the next few years Roshi and I worked together like partners, to expand the program of the zen group.

After a few years of zen training under the compassionate and gentle guidance of my first zen master, I began to discover the source of some of my dissatisfaction. It seemed to me that my environment didn't give me the right background to express myself fully. It was an environment in which I could express my parents' image of me, and my children's image of me, and my friends' image of me, and even my zen master's image of me, but it wasn't a background in which I could express my own image of myself. The problem was that I didn't really know myself. All the images I had of myself were just that—images. In order to find out who I really was—in order to find my real self—it was necessary to allow myself a period of exploration, a period of wandering, a period of *apratistha*. It wasn't that there was anything intrinsically wrong with the environment in which I was living. It's the right environment for some. But my mind had turned the place into my old hometown.

I am convinced now of what I only suspected then— that the right environment is so important in the practice of zen meditation that it should be included in the Middle Way, Buddha's Noble Path of Right Living. Buddha's Old Middle Way contains eight steps: right thought, right intention, right speech, right action, right livelihood, right effort, right mindfulness, and right meditation. Buddha's New Middle Way would add the step of right environment— right in the middle of the Middle Way—between the steps of right action and right livelihood.

Before I could look for the right environment to find my real self, I first had to get rid of the web of karmic attachments that bound me to my old hometown. The word karmic is an Anglicized adjective form of the Sanskrit word *karma*. *Karma* is the physical-spiritual law of action and reaction. Karmic reactions are produced by actions that have a motive, actions that seek a result. Purposeful actions create attachments to people, places, things, and ideas. Purposeless actions don't create any future karmic attachments.

Take writing a book, for instance. If the book is written only to make money, or to achieve fame, the writer will create future *karma* for himself—"good" *karma* if the book is a success, or "bad" *karma* if it fails. (Both good and bad *karma* create problems.) But if the book is written for the sake of itself, just because the writer is *moved* to write it, it won't matter to him whether it is a success or a failure. The book won't create any future karmic attachments.

During my early years of zen training, under the guidance of Suzuki Roshi, I learned that *zazen* practiced for the sake of itself, and not for the sake of gaining enlightenment or peace of mind, was one of the most effective ways of getting rid of old karmic attachments. I didn't succeed (I still haven't) in eliminating *all* my old *karma*, but I *did* succeed in getting rid of some of my stickiest attachments.

One day, during a private interview, Suzuki Roshi told me he thought I should join the Zen Buddhist order. He wanted me to become ordained, and to wear the Zen Buddhist robes. At first I was shocked and disturbed. I didn't want to consider such a possibility until after all my children were grown and on their own. I still had two teen-agers living at home. I found myself between a rock and a hard place (or, as Buddhists would say, between two iron mountains). I couldn't decide which responsibility was the most important, the one I owed to my children, or the one I owed to that still, small voiceless voice, the "voice" that began urging me to give up everything and follow the path of the Buddha. (Shakyamuni Gautama, later to become the Buddha, left his palace, his subjects, his wife, and his child, to become a homeless wanderer. Buddha wanted to find an environment in which he could settle his mind and solve the problem of human suffering.) After much painful soul-searching I decided to leave home. The question of whether or not to become ordained was a matter I would decide later.

Suzuki Roshi didn't encourage me to leave home, or to give away all my possessions. But when he found that I was determined to do so he reluctantly accepted my decision. He felt troubled by my plan to give my home to the zen group. He tried to talk me out of burning my bridges behind me. But I was stubborn. The gift was made, not entirely out of generosity, but partly from my desire to be free of all ties to my past. Many of my friends, and some of my family, thought I would regret my decision later. I haven't yet.

This may be a good place to assure you that authentic Zen Buddhist priests never engage in the kind of con games practiced by many American cult leaders. Zen masters do not try to break up marriages or families. They never try to persuade members of their congregations to turn over their homes, cars, or life savings to the organization. Zen masters give their teaching freely. Only voluntary donations of money and time are accepted. Any zen master who engages in questionable cultlike practices isn't really a zen master. He is an imposter.

Eventually I was able to transfer my responsibilities to other capable shoulders. My ex-husband took custody of our two youngest children. Lester Kaye, an outstanding disciple of Suzuki Roshi's, took over my administrative duties for the Los Altos zen group.
When I had reduced my karmic effects to what I thought was the irreducible minimum (three cardboard cartons full), I left home. A friend promised to deliver these boxes to my first stop, which was to be a small cabin in the middle of a zen monastery in the wilderness behind Big Sur, California. On a brilliantly bright day in early spring I walked alone over a snowy mountain pass into my new life—at Tassajara.

Every two or three years, when Jack and I feel we are coming to the end of a period of zen life and are about to begin a new one, we visit the grave of my old zen master to express our appreciation to the spirit that points the way. We feel we are at one of those forks in the path now. So tomorrow we will leave Samsara, our trailer, in Big Sur and drive over the mountains to Tassajara.

II

The Center of Existence

From the canyon floor to the Quiet Place, the trail is steep in spots. Winded from the climb, we stand in the shade of a small live oak and catch our breath. This is an unassuming place, a small, shaded clearing on the side of a dry, chaparral-covered ridge. To ordinary eyes it is hardly more than a pause on the path before continuing on over the crest of the hill to find what may be waiting on the other side. But this is the place my zen master felt was the right environment in which to settle down forever. Actually, only part of Suzuki Roshi's ashes rest here at Tassajara. Some were sent back to his temples and family in Japan. And some were scattered to the pure winds that circle the earth.

We have no urge to speak or think. Our minds are relaxed and our bodies free to move in any direction. After our breath settles down to its normal rhythm, we lean our walking sticks against the tree. I put my hands together and bow in the direction of the natural *stupa* (memorial stone). The stone is two tons of unmarked, untiered, massive composure. I circle the *stupa* clockwise as Buddhists are trained to do. Jack circles it counterclockwise as he is moved to do. Jack is not a Buddhist. He doesn't practice zen. He never knew Suzuki Roshi during my zen master's last life on earth. But it is difficult to live with one of Roshi's disciples without becoming intimately aware of, and moved by, the living spirit of that remarkable man.

15

An animal has knocked over the vase on the altar stone. I set it upright. Jack has found a bamboo rake and is raking the sand in front of the *stupa*. When he is satisfied, he wanders off up the trail.

I find a can of incense sticks and put two short pieces in the ashes of the small bronze bowl. I light them. The smell of pine mingles with the smell of manzanita and wild lilac. I step back and feel my body bowing to the ground. I feel my forehead touch the earth. In the distance the deep toll of the temple bell calling the monks to midday service awakens something (someone?) deep within me. The boundaries between myself and my environment dissolve. . . .

It is not I but a black-robed monk who rises from the ground. It is not the bell but the earth that tolls. Everything is shifting. Now it is not a monk but the *stupa* that bows. Now a walking stick rises and bows again. Another walking stick returns with wild flowers and puts them in the vase. The *stupa* asks, "Are you ready?" The walking stick answers, "Yes." Two sticks of burning incense move down the trail that connects the Quiet Place with their new life.

A zen monastery is a particularly favorable environment to find ourself, to free ourself from attachments to old images and habits, to disrupt the routines of our old hometown, and to bring ourself closer to the true center of our physical-mental-spiritual environment. Suzuki Roshi was very careful to select just the right environment for intensive zen-centering. Roshi told me that when he was looking for a monastery site, many people tried to interest him in property on the tops of mountains—places that had majestic views. Most people thought this kind of setting would be ideal for zen meditation. But Roshi said that in practicing zen it was better not to be able to see too far. This is one reason he chose a canyon site. The physical geography of Tassajara, California, where Zenshinji Monastery is located, encourages zen students to turn their attention inward.

For a hundred years before it became a zen monastery, Tassajara Springs had been a famous old health spa. The name Tassajara is from the Spanish word *tasajera*, meaning meat-drying place—which undoubtedly refers to its American Indian and pioneer heritage. But if we translate the Spanish name phonetically into a Japanese near-equivalent, *taza-hara*, we might come closer to the awakened spirit of this particular environment. *Taza-hara* means to sit in the posture of *zazen* in the center of existence. *Taza* means to do *zazen* wholeheartedly. *Hara* is the abdominal center of the body, as well as the center of the whole zen environment.

The dirt road leading to Tassajara is narrow, steep, and winding. In summer it is dusty, and in winter it is frequently blocked by snow and rock slides. The road begins in the fertile valley of Carmel and ends in the most inaccessible parts of the Santa Lucia Mountains.

Tassajara was my zen womb. During the two years that I lived at the monastery, the high rocky walls of the canyon formed the pelvic bones of my zen environment, the monks and priests its soft uterine lining, the monastic schedule the strong uterine muscle, the beat of the great drum in the meditation hall the rhythm of its heart-mind, and the cascading song of the canyon wren the hint of other awakenings.

In the womb one dies to an old life. Old images and old attachments gradually, or suddenly, fall away. The ego experiences this period as a loss. Zen liberation is not a liberation *of* the self, but *from* the self. And so the return to the womb of the zen environment becomes a mixture of loss and gain, hope and despair. It is a period of intensified frustration between what-is and what-we-wish-it-was.

When I met my second zen master, Ryosen Tatsugami Roshi, I had been living at Tassajara for about a year and was growing dissatisfied with my zen progress. I didn't realize it then, but this was one sign that I was ripe for the second stage of zen practice. I was unconsciously looking for another zen master to help me through this phase.

Tatsugami Roshi was, I would estimate, in his middle sixties when he came to America at the invitation of Suzuki Roshi to lead two training periods at Tassajara. Besides being abbot of his own Zen Buddhist temple complex in Japan, Tatsugami Roshi had been, for twelve years, head training monk at Eiheiji, the largest Zen

Buddhist monastery in Japan. He had an imposing physical appearance and a virile personality. In his younger days he had been a champion *sumo* wrestler.

After a couple of months of watching Tatsugami Roshi from a distance, I told Suzuki Roshi that I felt moved to ask him if I could become his disciple. Suzuki Roshi encouraged me. So, on my forty-seventh birthday, I proposed this idea to Tatsugami Roshi, and he answered without hesitation (through an interpreter as he didn't speak English): "Since it is your birthday, I cannot refuse."

This was in March. Tatsugami Roshi planned to spend the summer months in Japan, returning to Tassajara in the fall for the winter training period. Before he left he announced to me that, when he returned, he would bring my robes so that I could be ordained. (At that moment I caught sight of the top of the mountain.) Then he wanted me to go to San Francisco to study the Japanese language in preparation for entering a Japanese Zen Buddhist nunnery. (At that moment I felt myself plunging to the bottom of the mountain.)

I had become attached to Tassajara—not to the monastic life or to the zen community, but to the canyon itself. The summer before, I had talked to Suzuki Roshi about my plan to stay at Tassajara until I felt some inner movement to leave—and Suzuki Roshi had approved. I knew I wasn't ready to leave the canyon yet.

I tried to picture the life Tatsugami Roshi had in mind for me. The thought of the years it would take me to learn everyday conversation in the Japanese language depressed me. And I was certain that one lifetime was not enough for someone as stupid as I was to master the technical language of Zen Buddhism in Japanese. I don't have a scholarly mind. I don't have a good memory or a talent for languages in general.

Tatsugami Roshi didn't speak English. As far as I was concerned, this wasn't a handicap. Rather, it seemed to me that because of the language barrier, he was forced to find more direct ways to reach out to his American zen students. And they were forced to find more direct ways to reach out to him.

I thought to myself: Words aren't zen. Zen transcends

words. Zen is communicated directly, from heart to heart. Sometimes zen *seems* to be transmitted by words, but actually the real message lies behind the spoken words or between the lines of the written words.

The thought of doing time in a Japanese nunnery was also depressing to me. To me, a Japanese nunnery represented a submission of the female spirit to the male chauvinist religious tradition. Although Buddhist scriptures have always proclaimed that there is no difference between the Buddha-nature of a man or a woman, in practice (I had heard on excellent authority) Japanese nuns have too often been treated like second-class Buddhas.

But the most depressing thought of all was the waste of precious time it would take to complete the program Tatsugami Roshi had outlined for me. I didn't have that much time! Very early in my zen practice I had taken a vow to save all sentient beings (not just fellow humans). This vow is one of the four great vows handed down from Buddha to his followers. Buddhists normally take, and act upon, this vow consciously by helping others and doing good works. But in my case, the first time I encountered the vow in my study of Buddhism, I felt possessed by it. It was as if I had taken the vow in some other life and had forgotten it in this life. Then suddenly I was reminded of it once again. The vow is a mystery because it appears to be an impossibility. But still I felt I had to try.

I decided then that the only way I could accomplish such a monumental and unreasonable task was to break it down into something I might conceivably be able to handle in one lifetime. I figured if I could save one hundred sentient beings, and if each one of them saved one hundred, and so on, and so on, eventually all sentient beings would be saved.

I had no idea what saving sentient beings meant. I was quite sure that salvation in Buddhism was different from what Christians understood it to be. I left that problem to be solved later. The only thing I could do at that time was to throw myself into the practice of zen. When I did this the vow sank into the background, and I wasn't troubled by it consciously. But suddenly it had come back to haunt me. And I realized that I didn't have all the time in the world. In order to save one hundred sentient beings I would first have to speed up the process of saving myself. (By this time I had learned that no one else was going to save me.) But how could I save myself if I hadn't even found myself? And if I couldn't find myself here at Tassajara, how could I expect to find myself in a Japanese nunnery?

After the initial shock I plunged into a deep depression. But a few days later I rallied enough strength to carry on with the everyday activities of monastic life. I had a position of responsibility at the monastery then which was rather demanding. But the problem in my mind was demanding too. I found it harder and harder to give my work my whole attention. I experienced lapses of mental activity, times when my mind went totally blank and I couldn't connect with my normal, everyday memory bank. It was as if something in my mind was overloaded and was shorting out the habitual mental circuits.

Then another trivial incident—this time involving an American Zen Buddhist priest who insisted that I assume some extra duties—"blew a master fuse." I collapsed in bed the next day, physically and mentally exhausted.

For months I remained in my room at the monastery. Everyone had a different opinion as to what was wrong with me. The deep-rooted conflict became so frustrating that I even stopped talking. If I had been living in a more conventional environment, or if I hadn't had a firm background of zen practice, I might have allowed myself to be put into a mental hospital where I would probably have been treated with drugs. The "civilized" or scientific response toward problems such as I was having often seems to be: Do something about it. The natural, or zen, response is more often: Observe it uncritically. Let it come in and let it go out. Don't cling to it.

In retrospect, I believe my zen illness was caused by a kind of metaphysical impasse for which there was only one zen prescription: Metaphysician, heal thyself. Because of my excellent treatment at Tassajara—which was limited to providing me with meals in my room and occasional visitors, but otherwise letting me take care of my own illness—I was able to abandon myself to my mental breakdown and concentrate on what was going on, rather than worrying about it.

Looking back, I can see that what was going on was—as it is called in zen—the great doubt. Great doubt is the literal translation of a zen expression that is actually a kind of mental fixation. It is an intense, involuntary concentration on some inner problem or conflict. For years I had been fascinated and troubled by the problem of self. "Who am I?" The search for the original self, the source of the vow to save all sentient beings, was always in the background of my meditation. Now I had slipped into the center of that original self.

I had known intellectually that to find myself would be to lose myself. But I hadn't realized how attached I had become to my old self, and how disturbing it would be to lose it. Actually, I hadn't lost my old self: I had only lost my *image* of my old self. In place of that comfortable old image was nothing but—how can I describe it? A Vast Emptiness? An ancient power? A not-self? Even now I have trouble finding words to express the nature of the power that possessed me.

There is another zen term, "family shame," that might help to shed a little more light on the experience. Family shame means a zen secret that can't be talked about—not because the participants are sworn to secrecy, or because they are ashamed to talk about it or afraid to talk about it, but because it is almost impossible to talk about it. I found the experience impossible to talk about because I was entering the second phase of zen development.

I have pointed out that it is traditional to have three zen masters, each one representing a different phase of zen growth. Suzuki Roshi guided me during my Zen Buddhist childhood. Tatsugami Roshi introduced me to my Zen Buddhist adolescence.

The second zen master can be likened to a spiritual rival. A challenger. A tester. He encourages the student to come to grips with his self. Or, as it is sometimes expressed in zen, to lock eyebrows with himself. The encounter with our second zen master may resemble a battle rather than a duel because it usually involves other members of the zen family.

At the least, this adolescent zen phase is upsetting. The newly acquired Zen Buddhist conditioning reaches the stage where it has become as strong as the zen student's previous social and religious conditioning. The two ways of seeing life are at war with each other. At this point a zen student may drop out of zen training completely (because it has become too mentally disturbing). He may take up some other spiritual path. Or, on the other hand, the zen student may give up his previous conditioning completely and throw himself obediently at the feet of his zen master.

At the best, this adolescent zen phase is revolutionary, and not just to the individual personalities directly involved. If this battle is fought wholeheartedly, between a great zen master and a great zen student, it can revolutionize the whole zen environment. The zen master and the zen student both change.

And since, from the Buddhist point of view, everything in the universe is interconnected, this change has far-reaching effects. For instance, the effect of the clash between Bodhidharma, the first Zen Buddhist patriarch of China, and his disciple Eka was the beginning of a revolution (or evolution) of Buddhist beliefs in China. It profoundly affected the whole social and literary fabric of Chinese and Japanese life.

On a smaller scale: If I hadn't locked eyebrows with Tatsugami Roshi, this book would never have been written, and you wouldn't be reading it now. If this book leads you to explore the zen environment more directly, it may revolutionize your life and have a profound effect on everything you do. Even if I don't accomplish my vow to save all sentient beings in this life, someone who reads this book may find a way.

This might be a good place for us to take a break. If you are just beginning your study of zen, I've probably stirred up a few disturbing doubts in your mind by now.

Jack and I are back in Big Sur. We're planning a picnic for tomorrow. After a pleasant day in natural surroundings, our minds should be relaxed enough to make it easier to push through this next chapter.

III

The Hermit

After sharing our picnic lunch, each of us is moved to explore a different path. I follow a winding trail through the sagebrush to a bluff overlooking the ocean. Here is a place where some perceptive artist had started to realize a dream. A huge gray boulder, slashed by green serpentine and brilliant white marble, thrusts itself nine feet above the ground. The path winds around the south side of the boulder. On the ocean side of it, the earth has been dug out to expose another third of the massive rock. Nearby are two neat piles of smaller rocks. It's clear that someone with sensitivity and character had planned to build a small house here—long ago, judging by the way the weeds and brush have taken over.

It isn't difficult to finish the house in the imagination, to picture rock walls rising against the bank, a fireplace against the boulder, a cement and pebble floor, rough beam ceilings, slab siding, and a shake roof. Most of the wall on the ocean side would be glass. And there would be a deck extending over the bluff.

To the south the Coast Highway appears and disappears as it winds its way precariously along the ridges and canyons of the Santa Lucia Mountains. To the north only a short section of road can be seen before it, too, disappears around a bend. Occasionally the sound of a car can be heard above the rhythmic roar of the breakers over a thousand feet below. The ocean is calm. Below, close to the shore, the sea is greenish blue; in the distance it shimmers with brilliant dancing lights. On the horizon the dark sea melts into the paler blue of the sky. A delicate mist clings to the shoreline, softening the sharp edges of the rugged coast. But the sun is well over the mountains to the east, so the mist will soon burn off. Through binoculars, the lighthouse near San Simeon can barely be made out. A few miles south I can see the flat where a hermit lived in a hut with two walls and a roof.

I wonder where the artist who began this rock house is now. Is he still wandering around, trying over and over, and failing again and again, to find a place to build his dream? Or has he given up dreaming and settled down in his old hometown? And what about the hermit? Is the hermit still wandering around, trying over and over, and failing again and again, to find a place to realize a dream? Or was the hermit a dream?

Inner self is something very strange. And powerful. We might call this "self" our karmic core or our karmic nucleus. The quotation marks around self are very important. Even if I don't always put quotation marks around the word self, we shouldn't forget them. They remind us that what we ordinarily think of as our self is not really our self. To speak of inner self, or soul, or spirit suggests something that is too permanent and too substantial. Since the minds of human beings tend to become attached to the idea of permanency and substantiality, Gautama Buddha emphasized the idea of process, rather than substance or matter. We can consider our self from the point of view of some thing or from the point of view of some force or energy.

Actually, neither substance nor process can explain ultimate reality, so it is probably best not to limit it by using any word. It's just "＿." But then if we don't use some word, we are apt to overlook it. We might allow our whole life to pass, believing that the limited description of ourself formulated by the collective ego of our time and place is the only true one.

So "　" is named in order to help us become more aware of some aspect of its true nature. It may be called zen, or *nirvana*, or Buddha, or Mind, or *tao* (the way), or the Man of No Rank. All these words are only names for that reality which is beyond names and descriptions. One of my zen teachers, Dainin Katagiri Roshi, cautioned his zen students that even if they reached the source of the river they would never be able to understand the totality of the river. In other words, even if we find our self, we still can never understand the totality of our self. But this doesn't mean we shouldn't try. After we find our self, we may spend the rest of our lives trying to name, or describe, or express our self. Even though it is impossible.

Sometimes Suzuki Roshi referred to our self as our inmost request. This may be a very good name for beginning zen students to use because it doesn't frighten the ego as much as some other names are apt to. The ego is not comfortable at first with names like *nirvana*, names that suggest a complete extinction or death of the ego. A *dharma* brother of mine was once so frightened by a sudden awareness of his cosmic connection that he was afraid to continue zen practice. A premature awakening may be viewed by the ego as one of utter loneliness, instead of complete atonement.

When we arrive at the center of our existence, and are confronted with something beyond time, space, and reason, our logical mind breaks down. Sometimes it takes a long period of reintegration before the conscious mind is able to fully absorb and accept the ecological nature of our self.

During this period, I identified strongly with Shakyamuni Buddha. In some inexplicable way I *knew* that *I* had been the Great Hermit who had taken the original vow to save all sentient beings. And, in an even more inexplicable way, I knew I had also been all the spiritual descendants of Buddha. The whole line of Buddhist patriarchs was not just a succession of individual Buddhas but was the extended life of One Buddha. Since it isn't easy to live with someone who is suffering from mythic inflation, as I was, the realization that I was Buddha created many problems for my zen family, especially for my zen parents, Suzuki Roshi and Tatsugami Roshi.

Mythic inflation is a temporary and immature stage of spiritual growth. In the story of Buddha's life it appears immediately after Shakyamuni's birth, when the infant Buddha takes seven giant steps, points to the heaven with one hand and the earth with the other hand, and proclaims, "Between heaven and earth I alone am the World-honored One." Suzuki Roshi once pointed out that just being born into this world (or just being conceived) creates problems for ourselves and others, especially for our parents. But Roshi said that eventually these problems should be dissolved.

It isn't the identification with Buddha that is the problem. It's necessary to identify with the mythic nature of our self in order to experience it fully. One of the best definitions of myth I've found is by Marshall McLuhan: "Myth is the instant vision of a complex process that ordinarily extends over a long period." McLuhan explains that: "We *live* mythically but continue to think fragmentarily and on single planes." So we can't avoid direct contact with our original nature without shutting out the greater part of our self. The problem arises only when we become permanently attached to the myth. For we not only live mythically in the zen environment, but we also live here and now in the world of ordinary time and place.

The name I first used to express my innermost self was the Hermit. During the period that the Hermit was expanding my mind, and creating a new attachment to itself, it also pushed the monastic organization uncomfortably out of shape. The Marian problem, as my zen illness was called by some, disrupted the group life of the monastery. As far as the other students could tell, I wasn't physically ill. Naturally many of them couldn't understand why I was allowed to eat, study, work, and meditate apart from the other students. Since Tatsugami Roshi was in Japan, some of the students must have asked Suzuki Roshi to do something about the situation. But Suzuki Roshi (who was in San Francisco during this period) didn't choose to interfere.

When Tatsugami Roshi returned to Tassajara to lead the winter training session, everyone at the monastery hoped that he would find a quick solution to the Marian problem. But Roshi took his time. Except for one "chance" meeting in which we both just smiled and continued on our way, and one formal interview when I remained silent and Roshi spoke only one word, Tatsugami Roshi and I didn't meet face-to-face. It wasn't until the end of the training period, nine months after he had accepted me as a disciple, that the spiritual obstetrician used his Sword of Wisdom to cut the Hermit out of its zen womb and sever the umbilical cord that tied it to the organized community of Zen Buddhism. At least that's one metaphoric explanation of what happened in my complex inner mythical life. On the surface, in ordinary life, the only thing that happened was that Tatsugami Roshi ordered me to leave Tassajara—and I did.

Was being expelled a punishment for my disobedience, or a natural course of events in zen training? When an infant is forced to leave the womb of its mother it may *feel* like a punishment to the mother and the child, but actually it happens quite naturally. At the time I felt that Roshi's order reflected my own inner readiness to leave. I had finally lost my attachment to my zen womb. (My attachment to the Hermit would take longer to lose.) I was never officially ordained. I never tried on my silk Buddhist robes. It was to be my *karma* to go forth into the homeless state (as Buddhist ordination is described) wearing only my everyday clothes.

Before I move on to the other side of the Santa Lucia Mountains to Big Sur, where my *karma* was to carry me next, I want to say just a few words about the third phase of zen. I can't speak from personal experience about the third relationship with our self because I'm still not completely ready for it. But it may help us to recognize our third zen master if we think of Maitreya as the ideal teacher for this third phase of zen.

Maitreya is the Buddha to come, the future Buddha, or our innate wisdom-nature waiting to be awakened to full consciousness. It is interesting to me that Maitreya Buddha is not ordained to become a traditional zen priest. It is also interesting that the Sanskrit root of the name Maitreya is friendliness. A real friendship is not an easy thing to experience in this life. According to my understanding of zen, it takes years and years of hard work learning to accept ourselves completely, with all of our imperfections and all of our potentials, before we are ready to accept our own Maitreya Buddha-nature.

I feel that America is the right environment for the development of a more democratic and informal expression of zen. This isn't to suggest that Maitreya Buddhism will, or should, completely replace the older forms of Zen Buddhism. There is plenty of room in America for all kinds of Buddhas to express themselves, from the most traditional to the most iconoclastic. But sooner or later each zen student must decide whether he is called upon to be a follower of past Buddhas or to be a creator of future Buddhas. When I left Tassajara I had made my decision—to follow no one but my "self."

This afternoon Jack and I are leaving Samsara in the campground at Pacific Valley and will be driving south to Gorda Mountain. We plan to camp out overnight on the property where I lived when I first came to Big Sur.

IV

On the Brink of Nirvana

Morning crawls languidly out of its sleeping bag. The silence is profound. The only sounds are the flutter of wings as a small field sparrow flies close to the ground past the open end of the tent. There is no other movement. Everything else—grass, flowers, insects, trees, thoughts—is quite still. There are a few ripples on the surface of the ocean, but they are very small and very far away. Quietly and carefully I slip out of the tent, giving my camping partner time to enjoy his dream while I take time to enjoy mine.

Cold creeps through layers of clothing, touching the skin. It penetrates the muscles of the hands, stiffening the fingers so that it is difficult to button and zip. But the cold isn't unpleasant. It's just cold.

Gradually the earth turns. Slowly the morning manifests itself. First the mountains to the north are uncovered, their shadows swept away by the bright glow of the sun. Then color touches the edges of the hills and gullies and meadows until the whole body of the mountain lies gleaming and yawning in the bright beginning of a new day.

A little breeze stirs the grass. The mind moves gently, and the body moves slowly, attending to its morning tasks with as little thought or effort as the moving of a leaf or petal. The sweet gurgling melody of a bird, whose nest is hidden in the grasses nearby, is accompanied by the tap-tink of kettle and spoon as I heat water for a cup of tea and warm up a can of soup.

I carry my breakfast to a rock which overlooks the three thousand galaxies. But it is not soup that I eat; it's wild flowers, sourgrass, bay leaves, soaring hawks, craggy rocks, a passing freighter-with-two-masts-headed-north, and a red station wagon slowly climbing up the rutty mountain road. It is not tea that I drink; it is the deep blue sea, the clear blue sky, the bright gold sun; everything-I-see-and-hear-and-taste-and-touch-and-smell-and-think at this moment becomes a part of me and I a part of it.

In the bottom of my teacup only a white froth remains. I sip the slightly bitter foam, draining the last offing and more. I drink until I have swallowed the entire ocean and the ocean has swallowed me. Now there is nothing left but the blue Pacific.

In one of his books Carlos Castaneda tells of how his spiritual guide, don Juan, the Yaqui Indian sage, introduced him to the art of finding a beneficial spot. At first the student was instructed to try to find a spot in front of the door of the teacher's house which gave him a good feeling, and another spot which gave him a bad feeling. It took Castaneda most of a night to begin to become faintly aware of the different feelings emanating from different spots. After he gained more sensitivity, the student acquired the habit of getting the feel of larger areas.

This exercise, like many of the teachings of don Juan, is an excellent technique to help zen students become more aware of the right environment. The right environment, like don Juan's beneficial spot, is not a place to fall asleep or a place to get high; it is a place that awakens us to our full ecological nature. It might take us a lifetime to find the right environment, the place in which our inner and outer selves are harmonized and fully realized. We may never find the right environment, the perfect environment, the zen environment, but this is not really important. The important thing is that we try to become more aware of how different environments alter our image and our expression of our self and that we also try to become aware of how impossible it is to separate ourselves completely from our environment.

In China, in ancient times, many zen monks and poets took the names of their locales as their zen names or their pen names. The most classic example I can think of is Han-shan, who lived in the Tang Dynasty. *Han-shan* means cold mountain. Here are a couple of Han-shan's poems, translated by Gary Snyder, the zen poet who first introduced me to the practice of *zazen*.

> *I wanted a good place to settle:*
> *Cold Mountain would be safe.*
> *Light wind in a hidden pine—*
> *Listen close—the sound gets better.*
> *Under it a gray-haired man*
> *Mumbles along reading Huang and Lao.*
> *For ten years I haven't gone back home*
> *I've even forgotten the way by which I came.*

> *Cold Mountain is a house*
> *Without beams or walls.*
> *The six doors left and right are open*
> *The hall is blue sky.*
> *The rooms all vacant and vague*
> *The east wall beats on the west wall*
> *At the center nothing.*

Huang and Lao are Chinese sages, and the six doors are symbols of the five senses plus the thinking faculty, which is considered the sixth sense in Buddhism. Gary says that when the Chinese poet "talks about Cold Mountain he means himself, his home, his state of mind." Han-shan didn't just stumble upon Cold Mountain. He wandered and searched for many years until he found the place that reflected his inmost request, the environment that felt just right, the environment that he knew in his heart was the perfect one to express his own deep understanding of zen.

As long as we are living we are changing, and so the right environment for us at one particular stage in our development may not be the right environment in another. After I was expelled from Tassajara, my hermit *karma* moved me to Big Sur. While Tassajara had been the right environment in which to find myself, Big Sur proved to be the right environment in which to lose myself. Physically and spiritually, Tassajara and Big Sur are very close. While Tassajara lies hidden like a fetus in the secret-most parts of the Santa Lucias, Big Sur clings, like an infant, to the western tits of the coastal range. Big Sur is not really a town or a principality. Although it lies roughly one hundred and fifty miles south of San Francisco, its boundaries are as vague and vacant as those of Cold Mountain. Lillian Bos Ross, author of the famous novel of Big Sur, *Zandy's Bride* (*The Stranger,*) ventured into the spiritual wilderness region behind Big Sur when she said, "Perhaps Big Sur is not a country at all, only a state of mind."

Big Sur is an environment lying precariously balanced between mountain and sea, between flesh and spirit, between conscious and unconscious, between male and female, between life and death, between ignorance and wisdom, between heaven and hell, between *samsara* and *nirvana*. Everything in the outer environment of Big Sur magnifies the inner polarities of human nature and intensifies the current that flows through the ecological system. The state of mind of Bug Sur is not found in the head or in the heart. As it is in zen, the state of mind of Big Sur is centered in the *hara*—in the guts.

It had been in Big Sur, many years before, that Gary Snyder had first introduced me to zen guts—*zazen*. At that time the state of my mind was located in the suburbs of existence, in the region between my head and my heart, between my intellect and my emotions. It took many years of zen practice before I was able to settle down near the gut center of my own life. But by the time I left Tassajara, I was living fairly close to it.

My hermit *karma* led me, without hesitation, to the right place in Big Sur, the one which was in harmony with my own state of mind at that time. On the west slope of a mountain blackened by a recent forest fire, at the edge of a secluded meadow two thousand feet above the Pacific Ocean, I was led to an abandoned one-room cabin. Actually, the cabin was only two walls and a roof that leaked, but it was enough to satisfy my hermit spirit. A friend helped me carry three cartons of past *karma* down the slippery, narrow trail to the hermitage. Two of the boxes were full of attachments I was still carrying from my old hometown. One box, the heaviest, was a collection of religious relics and responsibilities I had accumulated at the zen monastery.

After my friend left, I was alone. The east wall of the Pacific Ocean beat on the west wall of the Santa Lucias. With nothing to protect me from my environment, it was not difficult to be at one with it. Many mornings I sat enveloped in cool clouds that drifted in and out of the small hut I named Half-Dipper Hermitage. I lived there for four months on the brink of *nirvana*.

In popular Buddhism, *samsara* is sometimes likened to a process of burning, while *nirvana* is the process of blowing out or cooling. Zen first stirs us up; it makes us more aware of our problems and our illusions, and even creates new ones. But zen also helps us become aware of our deepest karmic nucleus. The Buddhist vow to save all sentient beings originates in the karmic nucleus. *Nirvana* is the peace and calmness experienced when we reach this deep level of ourselves, and accept our *karma*.

While I had been experiencing the full fire of my karmic nucleus at Tassajara the summer before, the mountain where I found Half-Dipper Hermitage was also being swept by a fiery awakening. During the winter the burned-out Hermit and the burned-over mountain cooled together. And before spring, green sprouts began pushing their way through the blackened ground around the Hermitage. I understand that there are certain species of plants and trees whose seeds sprout only after a fire. Our Buddha-nature may be like a seed that grows in the ashes of our burned-over forest of illusions.

When the mountain was covered with spring wild flowers, my *karma* suddenly and unexpectedly encouraged me to leave the Hermitage. Perhaps I was becoming too attached to it, and if I had stayed I might have turned it into my old hometown. Even if we *think* we have found the source of our self, it is self-defeating, limiting, and, strictly speaking, impossible to remain at the source.

I took only a few things with me: my sewing basket, an

Indian blanket, a sleeping bag, a pack, and a few changes of work clothes. The rest of my personal *karma* I left in the care of the Big Sur scavengers who live off the discarded dreams of transients. After I had gone, packrats, friends, and neighbors picked over the bones of my old writings, my books, my personal treasures, my silence, my solitude, and my illusions until there was nothing left of what I had once called my self.

Self? If you go back, as I did once, you'll find only the ruins of a solitary retreat. Clouds drift freely now through the empty hermitage.

With no home where I could settle down, there was nothing to do except settle down where there was no settling down. For weeks I drifted around—with no aims, no expectations—supported and protected only by my good *karma*. I slept in fields, on beaches, in backyards, and occasionally in strange beds. I ate on the road and brushed my teeth in gas-station rest rooms. I was helped on my way by Buddhas driving sports cars, Buddhas driving pickups, Buddhas driving station wagons, and Buddhas driving diesel trucks. I was treated to breakfast in San Simeon by a traveling salesman Buddha, given five dollars in Topanga Canyon by a retired schoolteacher Buddha, propositioned by several horny Buddhas in San Diego, fed tortillas and refried beans by a *familia* of Mexican Buddhas in Tecate, threatened by a crazy Buddha outside Phoenix, and whisked to safety by a little old Buddha in tennis shoes; I was preached to in Provo by a Seventh Day Adventist Buddha, entertained in Reno by a banjo-playing Buddha, and spoiled in San Francisco by a hospitable Buddha.

A Buddha (one of my *dharma*-sisters) in Carmel told me that Suzuki Roshi was recuperating from a serious illness. He was at Tassajara. It had been over a year since Roshi and I had met for a heart-to-heart talk, so the next morning, after breakfast with my *dharma*-sister, I hitchhiked to the Monastery.

The Buddha who opened the door of Suzuki Roshi's room didn't look as ill as I had been led to expect. We greeted each other warmly, and Roshi invited me in. Since this was an unusual occasion, he said that we should first bow to each other. In the past, whenever I had come to Roshi's room for formal instruction, the disciple had bowed to the zen master. This time Buddha bowed to Buddha. Three times our foreheads touched the floor. Then we knelt at a low table and were served cups of hot green tea by Roshi's attendant. Neither of us felt moved to speak.

It was Roshi who finally broke the silence. "I looked out of my window the day before yesterday," he said, pointing to the small, sliding, paper-covered window behind his low desk, "and I saw you." (Day before yesterday I had been in San Francisco with no intention of going to Tassajara.) "But then I said to myself," Roshi continued, "no, that can't be Marian. That girl is too young." He smiled at me, and his eyes twinkled mischievously. "But now I can see that it *was* you I saw through my window."

I told Roshi how glad I was that *he* looked so well. He said that Japanese men often have their biggest health problems around his age, but if they recover from this critical period they live an unusually long and healthy life. We both agreed that Roshi was on the road to recovery and would live to a ripe old age.

Roshi asked about my own life. I told him that I wasn't practicing *zazen* at the moment, and I didn't expect to return to formal zen training, but that I was happy. I said that I was planning to go back to Big Sur because I felt that it was the right environment for me. I told him that since I had left Tassajara I had discovered that ordinary people, people who knew nothing about Buddhism, had a lot to teach me about zen.

Roshi listened intently, nodding his head now and then. "You are much more humble than when I saw you last," he said, "so the life you are living must be good for you. I can see that you are healthy and happy, and that is all that matters to me."

Suzuki Roshi had poured much time and attention into my zen training. He had hoped that I would wear the Buddhist robes and devote my life to teaching Zen Buddhism. But he let go of my life effortlessly—just as effortlessly as he would let go of his own life a few months later. Neither of us knew then that it would be the last time we were to meet face-to-face—in this life.

V

Drifting Clouds:
Flowing Water

Sheltered from the chilly north winds and warmed by the early-morning sun, the rocky ledge above the wild sea offers a perfect spot to clear the mind of yesterdays and tomorrows. The ebb and flow of the tide creates its own rhythm of life, its own time and space. Near the cliff's edge the water is churned into a frothy serpentine green. Huge waves crash against the rocks below, tossing milky white spray two stories into the air. Further out the ocean is a dull blue; the sky is baby blue. The horizon between is sharp and unbroken.

Offshore, a massive domelike rock is covered with pelicans. There must be a hundred. Most of them have finished their morning feeding. Bellies full, they are resting while their breakfast digests. A small flock of pelicans is still circling around a kelp bed where the fish must be close to the surface. Every few seconds one of the big birds folds its wings and dives straight down into the water. Then a half dozen seagulls (who have been waiting for their chance) swoop in like fighter planes. Popping out of the water a second or two later, the pelican is lucky if it can swallow its catch before one of the seagulls snatches it away.

It's a bit rough for fishing, but not too rough to discourage Jack. Wearing his knitted cap pulled down over his ears and his old dark wool shirt buttoned up under his whiskers, he carefully picks out his place on the north-west side of the rocks. He baits his hook and casts his line out to a spot well beyond the turbulent waters below.

Fishing is a form of meditation, one that is popular with a great many American men. Like many activities, fishing can be treated as a sport or an ego trip. But, at its best, fishing is a meditation. Pursued for the sake of itself, the catch is incidental, an extra bonus. The real catch is peace of mind, cleansing of the senses, and connection with the mythic levels of being. When a master of meditation lets down his hook, he fishes the four seas and catches serpents and dragons.

For several weeks now Jack has been casting his bait out for some work and a place to caretake. But he hasn't had one nibble. He isn't discouraged. He knows Big Sur is a good fishing hole. And he is a good fisherman. At times like this it is better just to sit still and wait for the karmic tide to change.

The fishing pole bends and jerks. "I got one!" Jack shouts. He quickly reels in the line. It's a kelp bass, a small *satori* (enlightenment), a *satori* that can be seen, smelled, touched, tasted, and digested by an ordinary person as well as a zen student.

Jack baits his hook and casts again. Soon the fishing pole bends and jerks again. Another bite!

"Yoo-hoo!" Jack sings out as he reels in the line. Another fish has hooked itself on its new life. Tonight two kelp bass will be reborn as human beings.

I first met Jack when I was living in Half-Dipper Hermitage, in the middle of my period of not talking. During that time, which began four months before I left Tassajara and ended four months after I arrived in Big Sur, I communicated, when necessary, with the few people who drifted in and out of my silent retreats by writing notes. Jack couldn't read. We each thought the other crazy. Even though Jack reads a little now, and I talk a lot, we still insist that it's the other member of the family who is the crazy one.

The second time I met Jack I recognized a possibility. Was it his brusque manner, his broken tooth, or the glint in his blue eyes that reminded me of someone I had known long, long ago? Bodhidharma! The blue-eyed, broken-toothed old barbarian—that's how his followers affectionately remember the First Patriarch of the Chinese Zen School.

But it was the third time that we met, after I learned that he had spent sixteen years of his "previous life" in military service, that I caught a brief glimpse of the Man with No Name, Rank, or Serial Number. "This is a man," I thought, "not to be measured by an ordinary standard." Like the sixth zen patriarch of China, Hui-neng, a great revolutionary religious leader who was also illiterate, Jack didn't understand anything about Zen Buddhism. When the Fifth Zen Patriarch was asked why he chose Hui-neng as his successor, the Patriarch replied, "Four hundred and ninety-nine out of my disciples understand well what Buddhism is, except one Hui-neng. He is a man not to be measured by an ordinary standard."

Book learning is often a great inhibitor to the understanding of zen. Technical facility, the ability to manipulate words and symbols, is often mistaken for wisdom. Literate people tend to look at life through a smog of words. Illiterate people tend to look at life in a clearer and more concrete way. Literate people usually look for answers in books; illiterate people tend to solve problems by using their own horse sense or innate wisdom. These days Western culture tends to overemphasize the value of literacy and shows little respect for the illiterate or functionally illiterate person. Neither is more valuable than the other. They complement each other like husband and wife; a balanced culture needs to respect both talents.

Between our second and third meetings Jack and I both drifted away from Big Sur, I as far south as Tecate, Mexico, and he as far north as the Forks of Salmon, California. As in human love affairs, a vacation from the potentially right environment helps one to distinguish true love from infatuation. When Jack and I returned to the center of our existence, we found ourselves sharing the same spot—the place where there is no settling down.

Big Sur has been the practice ground for many nameless zen monks, though they may not have realized it. It is possible to be a zen monk, or even a Buddha, without realizing or accepting the fact. Many residents of Big Sur live a transient life, drifting like clouds, flowing like water, possessing no real property—scavengers living off the surplus of an affluent society.

The Japanese name for a zen monk, both male and female, is *unsui*, which means literally cloud-water. *Unsui* is a contraction of *gyoun-ryusui*, which means drifting clouds, flowing water. A zen monk, or a zen student, must be able to detach himself like a cloud from the confusions and frustrations of the ordinary life-mind of the samsaric world and float free and solitary as a cloud in the calm, peaceful life-mind of the nirvanic realm. In their cloud-water lives, zen practitioners experience many of the conditions, or states of mind, expressed by the Sanskrit words *nirvana* and *samsara*. Eventually zen practitioners integrate and transcend both the condition of being (known as *samsara*) and the condition of non-being (known as *nirvana*). The Middle Way of Buddhism is not a compromise between opposing concepts; it is a transcendence of all concepts.

In the cloud-water life, the zen practitioner moves in and out of both worlds. Tentatively speaking, original nature is *nirvana*, and human nature is *samsara*. Man's thinking mind is the source of his confusion and frustration, so usually the best environments to experience *nirvana* are those that contain a great deal of original nature, such as deep forests, high mountains, deserts, or oceans. In these natural surroundings it is usually easier to let go of the mental entanglements that distract us from our ecological connection with original nature.

During our Big Sur cloud periods, Jack and I lived high on the ridges of the Santa Lucias, in a variety of loose-structured structures: a tack house, a tent, a tin shed, a cabin, and sometimes in our trailer Samsara. The backcountry is a particularly favorable environment to disconnect one-self from the high-voltage wires of overcivilized conditioning. All of the buildings in which we lived in our cloud life in Big Sur have had the advantage of just one room. Mentally and physically, civilization tends to compartmentalize

our life and our way of thinking. Returning to the original
shelter of man, which has always been one room, gives us
a chance to reintegrate our physical-mental life.

Jack showed me how to improve the basic survival skills
I had acquired by-gosh and by-golly when I lived alone.
He encouraged me to throw away my books and taught
me how to read the tracks of his own zen teachers. The
earth and the sea were Jack's first two masters. The
animals, and birds, and trees, and plants, and stones
were his teachers.

Accustomed to the cement sidewalks of civilized life
and the raked paths of religious life, I felt like a two-year-
old toddling for the first time on the rough ground of
reality. But after a couple of years I learned to walk. I
learned other things too: how to split wood, trim wicks,
harvest miner's lettuce, pot-roast tree squirrel, pluck mountain quail, pan-fry sourdough bread, dry deer meat, brew
homemade wine. And I learned how to pick the bones of
city slickers.

Most backpackers, hunters, and spiritual gold seekers
enter the wilderness regions overloaded. Jack and I seldom find it necessary to buy clothes, or household items,
or parts for our old trucks. The Big Sur "Goodwill and
Old Parts Yard" takes care of most of our needs. Today
I'm wearing a pair of jeans I found hanging from a tree
alongside a hot, dusty road. The shirt and shoes were left
behind by a Big Sur dropout who returned to the city. The
totem animals of Big Sur are the packrat and the vulture.
Even wealthy property owners collect and trade junk left
behind by Big Sur tourists.

Settling down in original nature is not easy. *Nirvana*
contains just as many problems as *samsara*. The biggest
problem in both worlds is the thinking mind. One day,
before I left my old hometown, I drove Suzuki Roshi to
Big Sur. The day was clear and bright. Roshi was enchanted
by the spectacular coastal scenery. He told me it cleared
his mind of all thought. "But," he added (perhaps as an
intuitive forewarning to me), "if I lived here I would begin
thinking again."

When human beings bring their dualistic thinking mind

into the pure, unspoiled environment of original nature, *nirvana* often turns into *samsara*. Boredom and apathy are the mosquitoes and deer flies that drive us out of the wilderness areas of human nature into the comforting, pest-free protection of our old hometown. Freedom and independence are the wood rats that gnaw their way into our most well-constructed stash boxes of essential illusions and build their nests in the down lining of our sleeping awareness. The cloud life has its dark as well as its light sides.

One winter, when Jack and I were caretaking a remote cabin in the mountains behind Big Sur, we found it necessary to move down to the coast and live in Samsara for a few months in order to earn a little money to fill the gas tank of our truck and stock the shelves of the cabin. A few weeks later it began to snow. More snow fell on the mountains behind Big Sur than had fallen for many years. The snow broke the branches of trees. It crushed two storage sheds near our cabin. And then a wind came and tore the tin off the cabin roof and broke some of the windows.

Two times we tried to hike in to our cabin to rescue our cat. Both times we had to turn back. By the time we did get to the cabin, the cat had gone on—to Buddha's pure land, I hope. Then the final blow of karmic accounting. A down redwood tree that Jack was cutting (which he didn't realize had been pushed into a slight bind between two other standing trees) suddenly snapped when he cut through it, hitting his right leg and breaking the bones. It became quite clear to us that it would take much longer than a few months before we would be able to leave Samsara.

Jack is pretty tough. He is a fighter who is used to losing. He has learned to accept the breaks of the game without complaining. But breaking the bones in his leg broke something in his mind. It wasn't just an ordinary accident. One evening, shortly after he got out of the hospital, he spilled out some of the marrow of his zen bones to me.

"The most fun I ever had in my life," he began, "was the time I went on vacation with my mom and dad up to the south fork of the Salmon River—to Aunt Mabel's old cabin. Aunt Mabel panned gold for a living. Her nickname was Gold Pan Liz. The cabin had a back porch on it that overlooked the creek. And the first thing I had to do when I got there was get the ax out of my old man's car. He always kept it sharp. I trimmed the branches of a tree on the wrong side—on the side that was nearest to me. I gave the branch a good whack, and the ax came around and hit me in the leg—cut clear down to the bone. I started yelling, and my old man came and took care of me. I passed out a little when he was taking care of me, but aftter he got me bandaged I came around pretty quick. My mom made me put hot Epsom salt pads on the cut and soak it with hot boiling water twice a day. I was sixteen then.

"I made myself a wooden crutch, and after I began to walk I went down to a stream where there was a sandbar with a lot of willow trees. I cut a whole bunch of trees about a half-inch to an inch in diameter, ten to fifteen feet long. And I stuck them in the sand and curved them and bent them over like the keel of a boat. And I made the ribs by sticking them in the ground about three feet apart, bending them over and cutting them and wiring them together. I made the boat about ten feet long and about four feet wide. Then I pulled the whole damn thing out of the sand, turned it upside down, put a big piece of waterproof canvas over it, and wrapped the canvas over the chines [ribs]. I put other chines inside to hold the canvas in, and then I tucked the canvas in good and tight. This took me three weeks. Then I made a paddle. That took me two more days. Then I got in the damn thing and got ahold of the paddle, kept my legs straight out in front of me in the bottom of this canvas canoe, and paddled around the rapids having a hell of a good time."

There is a long pause while we both paddle around in our imagination having a hell of a good time. Then Jack pulls his boat up on the other side of the river. His voice changes from wistful to confident: "This accident is the best thing that ever happened to me in my life. My whole life has been nothing but accidents. I think it was an accident that I was even conceived. I was born prematurely. No one thought that I'd live. That I did was probably just an accident. Do you know something? My mind absolutely changes and comes alive when I have an accident."

Jack isn't accident-prone. In fact, he has had very few physical accidents in his life, considering the varieties of dangerous activities he has undertaken. That may be why I was moved to look deeper into this matter of his "accident."

To most people, an accident is something that just happens by chance. But to a Buddhist, nothing happens by chance. The law of *karma* applies to our spiritual or mythical lives as well as our physical or personal lives. Karmic justice is a complex process, but usually we only see the actions and reactions, or the causes and effects, fragmentarily and on a single plane. That's why *karma* appears to the ordinary person to be haphazard and accidental. It is only when we touch directly the mythic level of our being that we can occasionally glimpse the whole sweep of karmic activity that our ordinary minds only perceive over a long period of time.

Stubborn minds need drastic treatment to wake them up. The great Chinese zen master, Ummon, didn't come alive until his master pushed him out of the monastery gate and shut it so quickly that it broke Ummon's leg. Later Ummon founded his own school of zen. When a monk asked Ummon, "What is Buddha?" Ummon answered, "A shit-stick!" When another monk asked Ummon what was the teaching of Ummon's zen school, Ummon said: "My skin is dry and my bones are sticking out." For some reason—probably because he was so stubborn—Ummon's zen school declined and isn't thriving today. Ummon needs drastic treatment to wake him up. His skin and bones are still floating around in the Vast Emptiness. But someday he will wake up, accidentally, to his original nature. Then Ummon will raise his famous shit-stick again and revive his Zen School of Hard Knocks.

VI

Everything Is Buddha-Nature

I t is said that Buddha attained enlightenment at the break of the seventh day of meditation under the Bodhi Tree when he saw the morning star and realized, for the first time, its original nature. At the same moment he realized his own original nature and the original nature of everything in his environment. Whenever our Buddha-nature awakens from its spiritual sleep, we realize that everything has innate wisdom-nature like our own. Buddha realized intuitively the true nature of life and the ecological interconnection of awareness. A few scientists have just recently begun to wake up to the realization that not only animals but plants and even minerals may have some degree of awareness, intention, and feeling. Of course, children and poets and mystics have told us this for a long time. Everything—animal, vegetable, and mineral—has sentient being, capable of being awakened by us and capable of awakening us.

It is impossible to separate ourselves from our environment. Of course, we have some power over our environment, but our environment has some power over us too. It is a mutual relationship. It is a mutual exploration. It is a problem of finding not only the right environment, but finding the right position in our environment. Whenever we move into a new environment, we change the existing balance. Everything resists change. Even the animals and the inanimate things like stones and houses and pieces of junk have positions in the environment.

Any change in the environmental balance will be resisted a little, or a lot, depending on each object's particular attachment to its position. A stone, for instance, has an attachment to the ground. We could say that this is the ego of the stone. A stone resists being lifted from the ground. A small stone has less attachment or ego than a big stone. Fire has an attachment to fuel and air. If you deprive fire of fuel or air, it will sulk and hide itself. If you give fire too much fuel or air, it will get carried away with itself. Animals have attachments to particular places. And certain places have attachments to certain animals. Environments that give animals fulfillment in the right types of food, in the right kinds of shelter, and in the right opportunities for expression form strong attachments to the animals who live in them. And when animals find a satisfying environment, they will fight with all their power to hold onto that environment and try to keep intruders out of it.

When I first began to live in Half-Dipper Hermitage, I had a struggle to establish my right to live there. The packrats that lived in the cabin were used to having the whole place to themselves. They resisted me. I took away some of their space and some of their freedom. Every night the biggest rat ran around and around the small room, knocking dishes off the shelves and thumping its tail to let me know I was not welcome. The packrats had become a little too attached to that particular environment. They thought they owned it. But no one owns anything. We don't even own ourselves.

I caught the rats in a cage, one by one, and carried them to a place about a mile away and let them go. I knew that they would find a way to survive in their new environment, just as I had found a way to survive when I got caught in a cage of my own making at Tassajara and my *karma* carried me to a new environment on the other side of the mountains.

Because I was stupid I made the same mistake in the Hermitage in Big Sur that I had made in the Monastery at Tassajara. I tried to remodel it, instead of letting it remod-

el me. So original nature reappeared to teach me the old
lesson over again. I came home one day to the Hermitage
after a begging trip to the County Welfare Office, and
found that someone from the County Health Department
had paid me a visit while I was away. There was a note
tacked on the door. In large official letters it said:

CONDEMNED BY THE
MONTEREY HEALTH DEPARTMENT

Such a beautiful little cabin too. It had so many spiritual
advantages. But it failed to pass the county health standards. It didn't have the material advantages of hot and
cold running water or a flush toilet. When I moved out,
the owner had the cabin torn down. And the pile of old
boards that were left became the kind of environment
totally satisfying to a packrat's inmost request. The last
time I revisited the place, the original occupants had
converted the pile of boards into a packrat commune. It
made me wonder if human beings really *are* the most
intelligent species on earth.

Enlightenment, awakenment, or waking up to our original nature does not happen just once. As human beings
we all have a tendency to fall asleep over and over. And
so we have to wake up again and again. Although we are
all Buddhas, there are more sleepy Buddhas in this world
than awakened-again Buddhas. When I read the condem-
nation sign on the door of Half-Dipper Hermitage, I was
reminded that even though I was Buddha, the officials of
the County Health Department were also Buddha. There
is a tendency among zen students to consider administra-
tors, public officials, and politicians to be lacking in spiritual awareness. But Buddha often appears in the most
unsuspected disguises and unlikely forms. Wherever we
turn, our environment is trying to teach us something.
There is no use trying to escape. If we don't learn the
lesson the first time around the wheel of *samsara*, we will
be asked to repeat the lesson over again. And we will
keep working on that same lesson until it penetrates our
skin, our flesh, and our bones clear down to the marrow.

And when that happens, we wake up to the realization that *everything* is Buddha-nature.

But it isn't enough just to say, "Oh yes, I understand; everything is Buddha-nature," and think that by learning the words we have learned the lesson. We must experience the lesson deeply and repeatedly. I still have many more "classes" to take before I realize the fact fully and completely. Every now and then something in my environment reminds me in its own very direct, painful, or embarrassing way, "Hey, wake up stupid, and pay attention. Don't forget that I am Buddha too!" Yesterday I became so engrossed in trying to polish a paragraph on right mindfulness that I allowed a kettle of water on the stove to boil dry. The kettle was ruined. The worst part was that the kettle isn't mine. It belongs to the Buddha whose home Jack and I are supposed to be caretaking.

And now that I think of it, I guess that I've become so engrossed in remembering some of my past lives that I've forgotten to mention that our new caretaking job finally arrived. It's a charming house perched halfway up a wooded coastlands canyon, like a bird's nest in a pine tree. The owner is away on vacation and doesn't expect to be back for four or five months. Samsara is parked under some redwoods in a campground not far from here—just taking it easy.

Some odd jobs also turned up. Tomorrow Jack has promised to take me with him to a big ranch on the coast of Big Sur. While he is taking care of business, I'll be free to wander around the grounds. I've been to the ranch once. One of my meditation teachers, Gia-fu Feng, a contemporary Taoist sage, took me there one afternoon many years ago. Gia-fu wanted me to see the beautiful Japanese-style house and the old pond next to a bluff overlooking the Pacific Ocean. It's a zen environment my Japanese zen masters would have appreciated.

VII

Caretaker's Mind

A wisp of morning mist hovers, like a hungry ghost, over the calm surface of the old pond. Is it seeking a place to enter, I wonder, or a place to get out? Standing quietly on an outcrop of flat rocks I unhook my mind, like the small red boat that is tied to the end of the little dock, and allow it to drift lazily around this circle of silence. Slowly it swings to the left, as far as the golden body of Buddha rising above the tall pines to the east, and then slowly it swings to the right as far as the deep blue mind of Buddha crashing on the rocks below the spreading cypress to the west. Finally the mind settles down in the center of a bright green jewel of emptiness.

Graceful young trees, growing in a semicircle around the edge of the old pond, lean far out over the water, dipping their branches and trailing their leaves into its cool wisdom. Apart from the others, a lone willow weeps silently. A big trout leaps clear of its crystal palace; a small blue dragonfly disappears among the reeds. A swallow swoops over the pond and scoops up one drop of water from the source.

Walking slowly along the path that circles the old pond, I come to a low wooden bridge that crosses a small stream. I stand for a long time, listening to the sound of the water flowing under the bridge. Finally I hear my old master's voice speaking directly to my heart: "Please take good care of yourself."

When someone asks you, "What do you do for a living?" that person usually wants to find out who you are. We are what we do. Until we find a livelihood in which we can express ourselves completely, both physically and spiritually, we feel unfulfilled. And we don't know who we are. And so it is a good idea to ask ourselves once in a while, "What am I doing for a living?" In trying to find the right livelihood, and in trying to realize that livelihood fully, we will be moving toward the center of our existence.

As we grow older we may find that our spiritual point of view has changed, and so what once felt to us to be a satisfying livelihood may no longer fill our present needs. We may be able to perform our job skillfully, and the work may provide us with a good living, but we find that something is lacking. Somehow the work does not allow us to express ourselves fully. At that time we may look around for some more satisfying work, often to the distress of friends and relatives who cannot understand why we would think of giving up a good job or a potentially successful career which they imagine to be the right livelihood for us.

It was not until I began living in Big Sur that I found the right livelihood. (The discovery of the right livelihood often appears only after the discovery of the right environment.) At first I did not recognize that the work I was doing was my livelihood. Before I could become fully aware of my livelihood, it was necessary to approach it with the right effort. For a long time I looked upon my work as a means to an end. It was only after I began to look upon the work itself as an end that the work began to unfold its unlimited possibilities. In order to realize our work fully, we must do it for the sake of itself.

Another reason it took time for me to recognize my livelihood was because it was not accompanied by a salary. At first it supplied only a fraction of my basic needs, but as I began to give my work the right kind of effort it began to supply more and more of my existential needs—a little food, a little shelter, a little clothing, and a lot of zen life.

When I ask myself these days what I do for a living, I answer myself, "I am a caretaker." A caretaker does not own the environment in which he lives. Strictly speaking

he does not own anything, not even his body or mind ‹
life. A caretaker enjoys the environment in which he live
including his borrowed "self," and contributes to th
maintenance and improvement of his environment; but
caretaker is always alert to the danger of getting tc
attached to anything in his environment. I have found it
useful rule to live as if I were going to spend the rest ‹
my life right here, while also keeping in mind that I ma
have to leave here tomorrow morning.

In zen monasteries a great deal of time and attention
spent in becoming more aware of things and events whic
the ordinary person would consider trivial or unimportan
This develops the caretaker's mind. Most people in Ameri‹
have been brought up upon a diet of carelessness. W
have been conditioned to think that some things a›
important or valuable and other things are unimportant ‹
worthless. But in the world of zen—in the world ‹
original nature—there are no such distinctions as valuab›
or worthless, important or unimportant. Any incident ‹
any thing, no matter how humble or seemingly insignif
cant, may awaken our sleeping awareness.

When the Japanese *haiku* poet, Basho, heard the soun
of a frog jumping into an old pond, the karmic rippl‹
that circled out over the calm surface of the water extenc
ed on beyond the pond, beyond the earth, beyond th
moon, the sun, the furthest star, beyond space. And th
frog that plunged into the calm pool of Basho's mind san
deeper than Basho, deeper than Bodhidharma, deep‹
than Shakyamuni Buddha, into the realm of timelessnes:

Basho wrote a *haiku* poem about his simple experienc‹
a poem which has awakened and reawakened countle›
beings to the limitless realm of the ordinary, everyda
world:

> Old pond;
> Frog jumps in—
> Plop!

Perhaps it was the ripples on the surface of Basho's o›
pond that animated Suzuki Roshi when he spoke abou
frogs. Roshi often used frogs as examples in his lectur‹

on *zazen*. One afternoon I took Roshi to meet Gia-fu Feng, who was living at the time in a tiny hut built over a waterfall at Esalen. The three of us (China, Japan, and America) were a crowd in that tiny hut. Gia-fu showed Suzuki Roshi a book of Japanese prints, and Roshi laughed delightedly when he came to one of his favorite prints. It was a painting of a frog by Sengai, with the caption under it: "If by sitting in *zazen* one becomes a Buddha..." I often wonder if Roshi spent some of his earlier incarnations as frogs and if he occasionally wished to return to the simple life of a frog living beside an old pond.

The house Jack and I are caretaking this summer has a delightful collection of ceramic frogs. Since the owner gave us her permission to rearrange things to suit our own needs, I set up a little memorial altar on a glass-topped table. Around my favorite picture of Suzuki Roshi I arranged the collection of green ceramic frogs. The biggest frog has his mouth open. He is croaking a froggy chant while accompanying himself on a guitar. One frog reclines, like Buddha in his *nirvana* pictures; one frog sits with his hands crossed over his fat tummy and his knees up in a beginner's *zazen* position. Two very small frogs sit on a rock. They have their hands together, ready to dive in. When we put our hands together like this, in the universal gesture of reverence, greeting, and deep respect, we are getting ready, like these little frogs, to dive into Basho's old pond—to plunge into our own mind, the mind that includes Basho's mind, and Suzuki Roshi's mind, and Bodhidharma's mind, and Buddha's mind—in short, original mind.

The work of taking care of our environment also means taking care of ourself. When zen masters bid good-bye to their students and friends, they often say, "Take good care of yourself." When you take good care of yourself, you will take good care of your environment; and when you take good care of your environment, you will also take good care of yourself. You and your environment will work together harmoniously to reveal your original ecological nature. To take care of something or someone is to respect it fully, and to be completely aware of its true nature. Sometimes taking care of something or someone means to be careless—that is, to be careless about one's own personal reputation.

A fellow zen student, an exceptionally dedicated and talented young man, retains a vivid picture of Suzuki Roshi going through the door of the old Sokoji Temple in San Francisco, "rather carelessly, pulling the doorknob so that the door swung but did not fully close behind him." I haven't seen this zen student for many years, but I remember his constant effort to practice mindfulness. Whether it was consciously or unconsciously, I think Suzuki Roshi was attempting to show this young man the true nature of right mindfulness. Sometimes zen carefully closes the temple door, but at other times it carelessly leaves the door ajar. The difference depends upon the character of the zen student or the particular stage of his development.

There is a famous old zen story that underlines this attitude. A tea master asked his son to rake the leaves in the temple garden. When the boy was finished, the father did not offer his approval. The boy returned to the garden, taking great care to rake it thoroughly until there was not one leaf or twig to mar the perfection of the landscaping. But still the father did not give his approval. The boy did not understand; so the tea master stepped into the garden and shook a tree, allowing a few autumn leaves to fall upon the clean-swept ground.

In zen training one rakes or sweeps one's inner garden or character. But completion comes when the zen master shakes a few leaves upon the immaculate ground. The zen student who is striving for perfection may someday be a zen master himself. When the time is ripe for his promotion, he will probably encounter a great windstorm, one which will shake the Bodhi Tree in his well-groomed garden. Then the spirit of his departed master, who has been watching through the door he "carelessly" left ajar, will nod approvingly.

VIII

Cleaning Out the Corners

T aking care of our environment means getting rid of the old self, the false self, to make room for the present reality. Suzuki Roshi once gave a talk in my old hometown in which he said, "When you study Buddhism, you should have a general house cleaning of your mind. You must take everything out of your room and clean it thoroughly. If it is necessary, you may bring everything back in again. You may want many things, so one by one you can bring them back. But if they are not necessary, there is no need to keep them."

This lecture was suggested to my master the week after I had decided to convert my two-car garage into a traditional Japanese *zendo*, or meditation room. For about a year and a half Suzuki Roshi had been meeting once a week with a small group of zen students in my suburban home. Once a week I would move some of the furniture out of my living room and do my best to make it into a meditation room. One evening, as I was preparing the room, a thought popped into my mind: "How nice it would be to have a special room just for *zazen* and lectures. I wonder if it would be possible to convert my garage into a *zendo*?" I mentioned this possibility to Suzuki Roshi the next morning after *zazen*. Roshi was enthusiastic about the idea.

Before work could begin on the *zendo*, I had to take everything out of the garage. At that time my garage was stuffed to the brim with puppets, props, scenery, stages, and magic tricks. Puppetry was an old hobby of mine that had grown into a business. Since it was summer, I moved everything out onto the patio. When Roshi saw the big heap of childhood dreams spread out in the sunshine, he couldn't help but laugh. Here were all the scenery, props, and magic tricks of my old personality. In order for an authentic human being to develop in an authentic environment, it was necessary for me to let go of the strings of my imaginary self and get rid of the props of my imaginary world.

Since they weren't necessary to my inmost request, I gave away all my puppets and paraphernalia. The zen students in my old hometown began immediately to convert my empty two-car garage into an original *zendo*. Six weeks later Suzuki Roshi dedicated Haiku An. A Japanese *haiku* poem has only about seventeen syllables. *An* is the Japanese word for a small temple. Haiku An had only room for about seventeen zen students.

I must add here that even though it took only a few days to empty my two-car garage of its contents, and only six weeks to convert it to its original nature, it took many years of sitting in it before I could empty my two-faced (dualistic) mind of its contents and allow it to resume its original nature or original face.

Sometimes it is only necessary to remove a few weeds or a few cobwebs to expose the original nature of an environment. Weeding and cleaning are very meditative practices. When done with full attention, without daydreaming, these activities clear the mind of lots of useless information.

The first project is to get rid of dust catchers. Simplify! Simplify! Simplify! Gather up all the fussy things, all the fancy things, all the false things (such as plastic flowers and books that aren't worth rereading), and take them to the flea market. If our life is very busy we may want to pack away some of our more delicate treasures. We can bring them out on special occasions when we can give them the attention they require. Getting rid of outside dust catchers helps us get rid of inner (mental) dust catchers.

In Buddhism the ideas of soul, immortality, and the pairs of opposites such as good and evil, or life and death, are examples of mental dust catchers. Any fixed idea that has not been moved around for a long time creates a place where illusion can breed. A fixed idea is like a stove, or a refrigerator, or a bookcase. Underneath and behind fixed ideas are hiding places that can collect all sorts of mental rubbish.

Suzuki Roshi used to say that what was needed most in the monastery were people who were good at cleaning out the corners. The most perverting ideas are the ones that lie for years and years in the dark corners of our mind. Like spiders, they creep out while we are sleeping and spin their webs of illusion. Only when the mind is clean, in order, and uncluttered can the present moment be fully realized. If we hang onto past memories, trophies of our good-old-days, in time our mind and our home will be a museum instead of a place to encounter the present reality. The relationship between house cleaning, gardening, and mental caretaking is not just symbolic. It is very direct.

The last few weeks Jack and I have been doing some odd jobs for an elderly woman who lives near the house we are caretaking this summer. Since the woman has lived alone for many years, her environment is not contaminated by outside relationships. It is clearer than most. There is nothing fussy or extra in her home. There is nothing artificial or pretentious. Although everything is old, the furnishings and their arrangement have an unusual life to them. Both Jack and I noticed the harmonious blending of the woman's inner spirit and her house and garden. And this reaches beyond her property lines. When she stood in her garden yesterday, the halo of her white hair was reflected in a fluffy white cloud that floated in the blue sky of her extended environment.

When we started to work, the old woman and her old house and garden weren't feeling too well. She told us that she had let things go for some time because she didn't have the energy to cope with the involvements of people working in her sheltered environment. We had been recommended by a close friend as quiet and mature workers, so she had decided to try us out.

On the first visit the woman told us that the two tasks she wanted completed first were washing the windows of the house and clearing the paths of the garden. We washed the windows first. Jack washed outside, and I washed inside. That way we could catch each other's misses. (Which is, isn't it, what husbands and wives do best?) When the windows were clean, the woman was very pleased. And we could almost hear the house echoing her gratitude. "Oh, it's so *good* to be able to see out again." Houses, as well as people, suffer from claustrophobia and can infect the spirit of the occupants.

I began to wonder if there was an inner and outer connection between the woman's desire for clean windows and a cleared path. A window is something to see through. Eyes are windows. A path is a way . . . and then it came together. She wanted to be able to "see her way clearly." This is an expression we use when we have a difficult decision to make or accept. Perhaps her decision concerned her health or a family problem. The particular problem didn't concern me, only the relationship between the inner mental state and the outer environment. I predicted to Jack that by the time we had cleared the path she would be well on her *way* to the solution, or acceptance, of her problem.

And as our job progressed in the garden we noticed that the spirit of the woman became stronger and healthier each day. In a few days she came out of the house and began to give her potted plants her personal attention. By the end of the second week she looked twenty years younger; she bloomed like one of her repotted plants. On the surface not much was happening. Some windows were being washed. Some weeds were being pulled. But looking more closely, through the mind of a caretaker, it was possible to catch the delicate unfolding of a beautiful perennial plant, the flowering of her original nature.

From the position of renewed spirit, the woman was able to *see her way clearly* to open the door to the present reality. She realized that it was time to give up her solitude and independence. Yesterday she told us that she had decided to invite a younger relative to come and live with her to help her better care for her home. Our job was finished.

I think that the success of organizations such as The Salvation Army, in rehabilitating physically, emotionally, and spiritually unbalanced people may be due primarily to the intimate relationship between the activities of gathering, sorting, and distributing unwanted, cast-off materials and the activity of resorting and repairing the contents of the mind. Perhaps the increasing number of neurotic people among the affluent American middle classes may be due, in part, to the tendency to use machines to take care of house-cleaning and gardening tasks.

This may be a good place to bring up the general attitude of Americans toward work. Most people in this country have been conditioned to regard certain kinds of work as respectable and other kinds as menial. This is very unfortunate. It creates a lopsided cultural posture. In zen monasteries humble tasks, such as weeding the garden or washing the dishes, are considered just as holy as the esoteric ceremonies performed by the priests inside the temple. And the ceremonial activities, such as lighting incense or bowing, are considered to be just as void of holiness as digging ditches.

Younger monks in zen monasteries are usually given administrative jobs and older monks the humbler tasks. This emphasizes the equal value of all work. For example, a senior monk is given the job of garbage collector. And one of the eldest and most enlightened monks in the monastery is given the job of cleaning the toilets. The enlightening quality of doing such "dirty" work as cleaning toilets should not be underestimated. Not just because this kind of work teaches humility, or because it emphasizes the equal value of all work, but because a zen master will have many unpleasant or dirty tasks to perform in his teaching career. Like a psychiatrist, he will have the job of cleaning out the foulest corners of his own mind, and the job of helping his students snake out the clogged sewer pipes of their own minds. If someone were to ask me today, "What is zen?" I'd answer: "Zen is a plumber's helper."

If a zen master has any discrimination he will avoid the "dirty" work, and the quality of his teaching will suffer. So it is very important for zen students to develop the right attitude toward menial labor and to try to perform all their work, no matter how distasteful, with as much care, wholeheartedness, and reverence as possible. You can never tell. Someday when you are cleaning out the corner of some very old, decaying, dilapidated house, you might find a priceless jewel hidden in the dust.

IX

The Oak Tree in the Garden

B elow us the coast of Big Sur is still covered by a thick layer of cool fog, but at the top of the three-thousand-foot-high ridge the air is hot and dry. Summer is always hot and dry in the mountains back of Big Sur. But this summer the chaparral-covered ridges look as if they had been transported a thousand miles south.

It's the first time in over a year that Jack and I have been able to spend a day in the backcountry. We've borrowed the keys to the North Coast Ridge road from the owner of the property we were caretaking during the winter of the big snow—the winter Jack broke his leg. We drive leisurely up the dusty, winding road for fifteen miles and park the truck at Marble Peak. From the Ridge road it is a short climb to the top of the peak. To the east Tassajara lies hidden in the folds of the green and saffron-robed mountains. To the west Big Sur is hidden in the sleeve of a white-robed ocean.

Jack says he wants to hike down the east side of the mountain to Indian Valley. I feel moved to explore the west slope. I tell Jack I'll wait for him at the Marble Peak cabin which sits in a small clearing under a grove of pines, bays, oaks, and madrones a thousand feet below. The cabin looks just about the same as it did the last time I was here. It probably hasn't changed much since the man who was building it ten or fifteen years ago passed on. It

seems strange that no one has ever been moved to finish
the cabin, or that it has never had a live-in caretaker. I
imagine what it would look like after the rat turds and
trash were cleaned up. A few more windows would help.
I picture sleeping on the screened porch on warm summer
nights.

It's cool under the big trees. I walk around to the front
of the cabin and sit down under a huge black oak. I am
aware of a peaceful feeling I had noticed the last time I
was in the neighborhood of this particular oak tree. This
kind of feeling may have moved Shakyamuni to sit down
and rest his body and mind in the shade of the great pipal
tree near Bodh Gaya in India.

Not a breath of wind is stirring. I had forgotten the
silence of the mountains—thick, rich stillness that is vi-
brant and shining. Not a bird or insect breaks the silence
until suddenly—AUMMMMMMMMMMMMMMMM—a fly
with a diamond-pointed cutting edge bores a hole through
the center of the silence, and I feel my mind slowly oozing
out through the hole into the Vast Emptiness.

When I come back to myself I am recalling, in a new
way, an old *koan*. A *koan* is a kind of zen problem that is
used to help zen students break out of the limitations
created by their rigid way of thinking and acting. This
particular *koan* goes something like this: A monk asked
the Chinese zen master, Joshu, "Why did Bodhidharma
come to China?" Joshu answered, "The oak tree in the
front garden."

Today we might ask Joshu why zen came to America.
Or we might ask the oak tree why it came to Bodhidharma.
Or we might ask ourselves why we came here. This *koan*
is a deeper form of the question we often ask ourselves:
"Who am I *really*?" Or "What am I doing here?" I have
been asking myself this kind of question for many years,
but today this particular oak tree seems to be the most
solid and yet at the same time, the most illusive of answers.

All of a sudden I feel very tired. Tired of wandering.
How wonderful it would be to settle down, even if just for
a few years, in the shade of this great oak tree.

*   *   *

This morning, back on the coast, the *koan* has taken on a new dimension. A wood tick that had dropped from the branch of the oak tree yesterday is attached to my body. During the night he made good progress fulfilling his original nature. After our morning coffee Jack helps the wood tick to pass on to Buddha's pure land. Poor tick. He drank deep of my crazy *karma* and will be reborn in his next life with some problems he hadn't bargained for. But I picked up a bit of new *karma* myself—the tick's head, which is still buried in my breast. My body will be given the opportunity to absorb a lot of wood tick wisdom in the next few weeks. And in the same length of time, the wood tick will be forced to accumulate a mountain of human ignorance.

A wood tick has something to teach us about zen. I once read that a tick's awareness is very limited; or perhaps it is more accurate to say that a tick's awareness is very concentrated or one-pointed. I think a tick is only aware of the smell of a warm-blooded animal. If I remember correctly, a tick has been known to live in a state of deep meditation, attached to a branch in a laboratory, for something like eighteen years—until it was awakened by the smell of a warm-blooded animal. Then it let go of the branch to which it had been clinging all those years and dropped upon its victim.

Human beings aren't much different from ticks. We are only fully aware of what interests us, or what activates our selfish needs or desires. But even in our selfishness we are expressing our original nature. A zen master may be willing to wait for eighteen years or eighteen hundred lifetimes—in a state of deep meditation—before he lets go of his patriarchal branch and drops into the life of a pure-blooded successor.

There is another zen *koan* that goes something like this: Zen is like a man hanging with his teeth onto a branch of a tree over a precipice. Under the tree someone asks him: "Why did Bodhidharma [zen] come to China from India?" If the man in the tree does not answer, he fails; and if he does answer he falls and loses his life. Now what shall he do?

Zen is like a tick clinging to the branch of an oak tree in

a garden on the side of a marble peak four thousand feet above the ocean. And a wanderer passes under the branch of the oak tree wondering, "What am I doing here?" If the tick hesitates he misses his opportunity, and if he responds he falls and loses his life. When the tick is clinging to his branch, he is not aware of anything except *nirvana* or selflessness. But when the tick smells the warm blood of a deluded human being passing below, the tick becomes aware of his original nature. He realizes instantly how to fulfill himself and how to express his wood tick nature. He lets go of his Bodhi Tree and drops onto the body of delusion—without a second thought.

In the practice of zen we learn to become more like a tick clinging to a branch of an oak tree. But we should always be ready to respond immediately to the question that is passing. And every sentient being is a passing question. When the tick responds, he does not think about where this sentient being will take him. If the tick is taken to heaven, it's all right. If he is taken to hell, it's all right too. That is not the concern of the tick. The only concern of the tick is to sink himself deep into the flesh and blood of his host and suck out as much delusion as he can swallow before he passes on to his final *nirvana*. If you were clinging to a branch with your teeth, over a precipice, and someone asked you, "What is zen?" what would you answer?

PART TWO

Settling Down in the Zen Environment

I

Bodhidharma's Answer

What *is* zen, or original nature, or Buddha-nature? Once when Gautama Buddha was preaching to a large assembly of followers on Mount Grdhrakuta in India, he tried to answer this question. Silently he held up a lotus flower before his congregation. Only one of his disciples, the venerable Maha-Kasyapa, who later became Buddha's successor, understood and responded, ever so slightly, by smiling. About one thousand years later when the Emperor Wu of China—who fancied himself a devout Buddhist because he had built many Buddhist temples, supported many Buddhist monks and nuns, and encouraged the translation of many Buddhist scriptures into Chinese asked the newly arrived and most famous Indian Buddhist patriarch, Bodhidharma, "What is the essence of Buddhism?" Bodhidharma answered by retiring to a small temple where he spent the next nine years in silent meditation.

We are what we do. *Bodhi* means wisdom, or enlightenment, or awakening. *Dharma* means teaching, or doctrine, or law. Bodhidharma is the practice of *zazen*. The practice of *zazen* is wisdom or enlightenment teaching. When we sit in *zazen* we become Bodhidharma, or wisdom teaching itself wisdom. When we practice *zazen* we limit our environment to the smallest possible space. In this space we sharpen our awareness and penetrate to the true essence of our original nature.

Even though we imagine that the deep forest, or the high mountains, or some foreign country such as India, or Japan or Nepal would be the best environment for practicing *zazen*, it would be a waste of time to go to those places before we understand more about why we want to escape from the place where we are now. Until we begin to know our present environment better, we will not begin to know ourself. And until we know ourself better, we will not be able to turn in the direction of our original nature. So the practice of *zazen* must begin in the middle of our delusion, in the middle of our confusion, and in the middle of our imperfect environment.

Three feet by six feet—the size of a *tatami* (rush mat)—is all the room you need to practice *zazen*. This is the space allotted to each zen monk in a zen monastery. The monk eats, sleeps, and meditates in this space. An inexpensive straw beach mat makes a satisfactory substitute for the more expensive *tatami*. Besides the mat, the other basic piece of furnishing you will need for the practice of *zazen* is a *zafu*. This is the Japanese name for a fat, round cushion about fourteen inches across. It is covered with sturdy black cotton. The *zafu* is placed at one end of the grass mat. It's to sit on. Or you can substitute any firm cushion you find available.

The purpose of the *zafu* is to raise the buttocks off the floor slightly, to provide the best posture for *zazen*. Instead of sitting on top of the *zafu*, one sits on the front half, so that the pelvis tilts forward. It takes quite a bit of experimenting to find the right height and angle for each particular physical-mental build. Beginners often use two cushions to ease the pressure on their crossed legs, and after a few months or years, when their body-mind has become more flexible, eliminate one of the cushions. If the floor on which you spread your mat isn't carpeted, you may find that you will need padding between your *zafu* and the mat. Without it your legs may suffer needlessly. The traditional pad made for this purpose is called a *zabuton*. It is about two and a half feet square, made of black cotton, and is about the thickness of a folded blanket. A blanket makes a satisfactory substitute for a *zabuton*.

Care and respect are important in handling and using

tatami, zafu, and *zabuton.* Everything is Buddha-nature. Everything, including inanimate objects, is helping us to find our original nature. So even when using substitutions, such as sofa cushions, folded blankets, or beach mats, we should remind ourselves that they, too, are Buddha-nature and should be treated with respect and appreciation. It is not only the objects that reside in the temple that have Buddha-nature. When you treat all objects in your environment with care and respect, you are realizing (making real) the true nature of your environment. This place, too, is a zen temple. I, too, am Buddha.

Before you sit down on your cushion it is a good idea to consider what direction you will face. In Soto zen monasteries, students face toward the wall. In Rinzai zen monasteries, students face toward the center of the meditation room. Since my training was under Soto zen masters, I sat for many years facing a wall. It is interesting to consider the Soto position of "wall-contemplation," as the Chinese term *pi-kuan* is usually translated. As far as is known, the practice began with Bodhidharma. Before the time of the twenty-eighth Indian Patriarch (in the sixth century A.D.), the Buddhism that had been transmitted from India to China was a very formal and intellectual affair. It consisted mainly of the practice of rituals and the study of the scriptures. When the Chinese Emperor Wu invited Bodhidharma to the palace to question the Indian sage on the fine points of Buddhism, the Emperor expected some kind of rational, verbal answers. But Bodhidharma's way was more direct. Bodhidharma emphasized the practice of *dhyana,* or zen meditation. Instead of giving lectures on Buddhism, Bodhidharma sat in meditation.

During the nine years that he sat in silence, Bodhidharma became known as the *pi-kuan,* or wall-contemplating *brahman.* And the pictures of Bodhidharma often show the rugged old Hindu sitting like a great rock facing the back wall of a cave. *Pi* means wall or precipice and has an association in the Chinese language with a high or unscalable wall. The steep rock walls of Tassajara canyon must have appeared to Suzuki Roshi as the kind of outer environment that reflected Bodhidharma's craggy mind. *Kuan* means to perceive or to contemplate. So *pi-kuan* may mean, among other things, to contemplate a wall or precipice in order to perceive its original nature.

A wall can be a barrier. A wall can be a protection. A wall often represents a problem. Most of us have a tendency to turn our back on our problems. Facing the wall is turning in the direction in which we will take responsibility for our own problems. Facing away from the wall may encourage us to seek help from someone else or blame some outside condition for our problem. So it may be better for beginning zen students to sit facing the wall. Of course, if you have a Rinzai zen master and he has you face toward the center of the room, this is a different matter. Then your master will be your wall.

There seems to be a slight difference of emphasis, at least in the beginning stages, in the Rinzai and Soto teaching methods. In Soto zen training, the zen master usually sidesteps your problem so that you are encouraged from the beginning to work it out for yourself. Working on your problem is seeing through it. Whenever I presented one of my problems to my Soto zen teachers—with the expectation that they would sympathize—my zen teachers would usually laugh and say, "Don't worry about it." They could see through my problems, which existed only in my imagination. But to me each problem seemed like an unscalable wall.

In Rinzai zen training the master may give you a *koan* as a problem to work on and may allow you to project your problem upon him. He may frustrate you even further by making your problem seem even bigger than you had imagined. This may go on for months or years, until you become dramatically aware of the way you make everything into a problem. And you stop. But before you stop you have extended your understanding of your "self." Both Rinzai and Soto methods arrive at the same end by different routes.

In the house which Jack and I are caretaking this summer, I find the only free wall space available is the front door. It is a beneficial spot to practice *zazen*. The house, built many years ago by one of the Big Sur pioneers, is made of pine logs and hand-split redwood boards. The door is almost four feet wide, made of one slab of hand-hewn redwood. Hanging on the door is a wooden plaque with the American Indian prayer:

> Grant that I may not
> criticize my neighbor
> until I have walked a
> mile in his moccasins.

Sitting in this place, I realize that walls are not always walls but can be doors. A problem can be a door opening on an opportunity. No matter where we find ourselves, no matter what walls we contemplate, those walls are ones that we have built ourselves, board by board, brick by brick, stone by stone, by our past actions, our past *karma*. Nothing happens by chance. Wherever we are, it is our *karma* that has put us there. And there is something in our present environment that needs our fullest attention.

Bodhidharma's practice, *zazen*, is the unscalable wall; it is the problem. It is the working on the problem. It is the solution to the problem. When we practice *zazen*, giving it our wholehearted attention, we concentrate on the real problem which is our self. After we take care of the problem of our self, we will find that outside problems will take care of themselves.

II

Approaching Zazen

I t's evening, about an hour before sunset. A bank of low fog hangs over the ocean just off the coast. We drive in the back gate and leave the truck near the big house where, many years ago, I first encountered zen. After teaching the students in his class on meditation how to sit in *zazen*, Gary Snyder promised us all a reward for completing two full periods. Sitting cross-legged through two *kalpas* (mythical periods) of *zazen* was the most difficult challenge I'd ever encountered in this life. But I was determined to see it through to the end. The reward, a cup of tea, was my first real taste of zen. I'm still not to the bottom of the cup.

We walk across the narrow bridge that spans Hot Springs Creek, past the little hut built over a waterfall that once was the home of a Taoist sage. We take the path through the vegetable garden, passing big beds of lettuce, chard, spinach, squash, parsley, cabbage, broccoli. Walking past the lodge, Jack sees an old friend through the window.

"You go on ahead," he says to me, "I'll join you later down at the Baths."

Strolling leisurely down the path to the Baths, my feet touched by the good earth *dharma*, my eyes filled with the vast sky *dharma*, my ears pounding with the great ocean *dharma*, my lungs overflowing with the pure air *dharma*, my tongue still tastes, and my mind still digests, that first cup of tea.

In the vestibule of the Baths I strip down to my birthday robe, washing it gently with sweet scented soap and rinsing it under showers of hot and cold water. Still dripping as it descends to the Bathroom, my original *dharma* body feels as formless as the ocean breeze.

There is nothing so depressing to me as being forced to take a bath cramped inside the ugly box of the ordinary western-style bathroom. Bathing is a spiritual as well as physical experience. So the bathroom should express its total function. Man originally bathed outdoors in streams and lakes. The Indians bathed here at Hot Springs in natural hollows in the ground. Later, tubs were added for the convenience of civilized men. And later still, rooms were built around the tubs to shelter sensitive spirits from the rough elements. But these rooms only have three walls. The west walls of Esalen's Bathrooms are nothing but emptiness. Here the original spirit of man can still mingle freely with the original spirit of nature.

I light a stick of incense. Stepping into one of the big fonts, I sink, like a tea bag, into gallons and gallons of steaming hot water. Slowly everything drops away and dissolves. . . .

At Tassajara no shoes or socks are worn in the meditation hall, not even in very cold weather. This may seem like an arbitrary rule. But the direct contact with heat and cold, one of the basic pairs of opposites, can be very enlightening. In ordinary life we usually try to avoid contacting the extremes and settle for a comfortable Middle Way. But Buddha's Middle Way does not mean avoiding extremes. Buddha's Middle Way contacts the full range of experience, finally transcending all experience.

I learned at Tassajara that the quickest way to get accustomed to the heat of the hot sulphur baths was to get in quickly before I thought about it. When just one part of my body was in hot water, it felt too hot to bear. But when my whole body was in hot water, it was quite comfortable. And just recently I had this same experience with cold water. Coming home from the day Jack and I spent in the mountains behind Big Sur we stopped at a forest camp called Cold Springs, named after its wonderful icy-cold mountain springs. As I was leaning over the big horse trough to splash cold water on my face and arms, Jack picked me up by the seat of the pants and threw me in the water. On the surface I was angry at him. I even called him several names I wouldn't want to put into print. But at a deeper level something was pleasantly surprised to discover that the water, which had been freezing to my hands, was refreshing and pleasant to my whole body. My mind was so shocked that it was transported beyond the pairs of opposites.

There is a zen story that Suzuki Roshi often liked to tell, about a monk who asked Joshu how he could escape the pairs of opposites: hot and cold, good and bad, old and new, man and woman, teacher and disciple, life and death, etc. Joshu answered: "When cold [be] cold; when hot [be] hot." Dogen Zenji explained further by saying: "When cold, be a cold Buddha. When hot, be a hot Buddha." In other words, become wholeheartedly what you are at the moment. When your whole body and mind are hot, there is no space left for comparisons. But when just one foot is in hot water, and your mind is comparing the state of your hot foot with the state of your warm body, then you are uncomfortable. This applies to all dualistic situations in life. If you are fat, be a fat Buddha. If you are thin, be a thin Buddha. If you are poor, be a poor Buddha. If you are rich, be a rich Buddha. If you are healthy, be a healthy Buddha. If you are clever, be a clever Buddha. If you are stupid, be a stupid Buddha. When all your energy is directed to the present reality, instead of being divided between the present reality and some past or future ideal, then there is no problem. And so when you walk in the monastery *zendo* in your bare feet on a freezing cold morning, there is no escape except in becoming one whole cold-soled Buddha.

Before entering the *zendo*, and before sitting down in their place of meditation, zen students bow in *gassho*. *Gassho* is the Japanese name for the ancient Indian expression of greeting and gratitude. In the position of *gassho* the palms are put firmly together and held in front of the body so that the tips of the fingers are about level with the nose. To make the bow one bends at the hips, keeping the back straight, without moving the arms, hands, or head. When a zen student bows to his meditation seat, before sitting down in the *zendo*, students seated on his immediate right and left respond by bowing in *gassho*. Even when they are absorbed in meditation, neighboring zen students acknowledge a student preparing to enter meditation by responding with a *gassho*. After bowing to his own cushion and to the students on either side of his cushion, the zen student who is approaching *zazen* turns to the right a half turn and bows to the zen student sitting across the room. This is paying his respect to all the other zen students and teachers in the *zendo*, and to all Buddhas past, present, and future. So even though you are the only one in your meditation room, you should still pay your respect, with *gassho*, to everything and everyone in the universe that supports your solitary meditation.

One of my zen teachers, Dainin Katagiri Roshi, often said, "The most important thing is: When you put your hands together you should do it with your whole body and mind." In one sense, when you bow before *zazen* you are preparing yourself for *zazen*. In another sense, *gassho* is another aspect of *zazen* itself. When right hand and left hand are together, two hands have become one. Passive side and active side are joined. Masculine side and feminine side are wedded. Conscious side and unconscious side are reconciled. Physical side and spiritual side are made whole (holy). It may be good practice for beginning zen students to keep their arms parallel to the floor during *gassho*. In this position the palms are forced firmly together instead of barely touching, which is our usual, half-hearted way of putting our hands together.

After bowing the second time, sit down on the *zafu*. Cross your legs. In the next chapter we'll give this "problem" more attention. If you intend to sit facing the wall, swing your body to the right on the cushion until you are in the correct position. With your hands resting on your thighs, palms upwards, sway like a pendulum a few times to the left and to the right, beginning with large swings and ending with smaller and smaller swings until you find your natural position in the center. Suzuki Roshi reminded his students that the practice of swaying before *zazen* and after *zazen* was not just preparation for *zazen*, or relaxation after practice, but was practice itself.

Swaying before *zazen* is life preparing itself for enlightenment. Swaying after *zazen* is enlightenment preparing itself for life. When we sway before *zazen*, we start with the widest arc our body will assume. Gradually we narrow down our attention and our environment until we concentrate on the area halfway between our extremes. Our right side and our left side are the pairs of opposites, the extreme range of our human nature. Until we know both sides of ourselves completely, not just our strong points but our weak points as well—until we have touched not only our own heaven, but our own hell—we will not find the right environment to settle down and penetrate our original nature.

III

The Mudra of Zazen

Just above a rocky beach there is a grassy knoll next to a small creek where I sometimes sit in the late afternoon. Here I can allow my mind to flow through the small willows, reeds, and grasses, over and under big and little rocks, until it mingles with the incoming tide. At the edge of the shore a huge black boulder sits half in and half out of the water. One white gull sits on top of the rock.

Today, while searching my mind for the essential nature of *zazen*, I realize that the black rock has been sitting much longer than I. So, in my mind, I ask the rock this question: "What is the essence of *zazen*?"

The white gull spreads its wings and rises on a current of wind, circles above and behind me, and then gracefully returns to its sitting place on top of the rock.

"Is that it?" I ask myself. (But it isn't exactly.) The gull rises once again, circles on the current of wind, and settles down on a neighboring rock next to five cormorants.

I don't quite understand, but maybe someday I will.

The physical posture of *zazen* is an almost insurmountable wall for Westerners, especially those over the age of thirty. I was over forty when I first began to practice *zazen*. During the first few months of trying to twist my legs into the cross-legged position, my knees refused to touch the floor. My posture looked more like that of a frog sitting on a lily pad than a Buddha. Three years passed before I was able to maintain a half-lotus position in reasonable comfort. During those first years of zen practice it was difficult for me to understand the statement of Dogen Zenji, founder of the Japanese Soto Zen School, who maintained that *zazen* was the comfortable way. I often asked myself why I continued to put up with the physical pain of the lotus posture.

Suzuki Roshi was very sympathetic with the physical difficulties encountered by his American students and never tried to force any of them to push themselves beyond their self-imposed limitations. My master encouraged older students to sit in straight chairs if they felt that the cross-legged posture of *zazen* was too difficult or too painful for them. But few of Suzuki Roshi's American students, even those over sixty, failed to make a determined and constantly renewed effort to sit in the traditional cross-legged position. Most of Suzuki Roshi's students discovered, as I did, that little by little they were able to accomplish much more than they had first dreamed possible.

Of course, the example set by the zen master is an important factor in motivating zen students to sit through the physical discomfort of *zazen*. Just as a child is encouraged to try to stand up and walk by the example set by his parents, so a zen student is moved to try to practice *zazen* by the example set by his zen master. To the zen student, the master is the living proof of the zen teaching. Shinran, the founder of the Japanese Shin-shu sect of Buddhism, expressed this kind of spiritual motivation when he said, "I do not care whether I go to hell or elsewhere, but because my old master taught me to invoke the name of Buddha, I practice the teaching."

But it is not only the influence of the zen master which keeps zen students from abandoning the traditional Buddhist posture. The *mudra* of *zazen* generates its own power. A *mudra* is a Sanskrit term which refers to a body position or a physical gesture believed to have magical powers. (The physical gesture of *gassho* is a *mudra*.) Actually, the magic power of a *mudra* is not something supernatural. It is an everyday kind of power. A smile is a physical gesture which has magical power. A smile is not only an outer expression of an inner state of mind, but it can, of itself, affect the inner attitude—not only of the person who smiles, but also the person who observes the smile.

The language of the body has been shown by psychologists to have definite effects upon human beings. Some of the messages communicated by body language are as universally understandable as a smile or a handshake. Others are more specialized, sophisticated, or less consciously explainable. The *mudra* of *zazen* manifests something beyond our conscious understanding. The *mudra* of the Buddha sitting in the full lotus posture expresses the deepest truth of Buddhism—to paraphrase Marshall McLuhan—"The *mudra* is the message." *Zazen* is enlightenment.

The figure of the crucified Christ is also a kind of *mudra* which expresses one of Christianity's highest truths. When a religious devotee meditates upon the figure of the crucified Christ, or the figure of the seated Buddha, the symbolic meaning of the images can be translated into many levels of his own life. But while the personal knowledge of Christ crucified remains forever beyond the direct experience of the ordinary person, the realization of the seated Buddha can be directly experienced by almost any human being who makes a sincere effort to assume the physical-mental posture of *zazen*.

Zazen is not a particular religious practice limited exclusively to Buddhism. The practice of *zazen* is the expression of truth before it becomes religion. Suzuki Roshi once told me that it was easy for a Buddhist to be a Christian, but it was very difficult for a Christian to be a Buddhist. I did not understand what he meant at the time. It was only after many years of practicing *zazen* and studying Buddhism that I began to make peace with my Christian roots and could feel comfortable with the message of the crucifixion. In Zen Buddhism the symbol of the cross, the transcendence of good and evil, is expressed externally and experienced internally by the cross-legged posture of *zazen*. So the most important thing is not the intellectual study of Zen Buddhism, but the direct teaching of the body language of *zazen*. This is why physical posture is emphasized by zen masters.

In Buddhism it is said that the sage touches *nirvana* with the body. In other words, Buddhism is not understood just with the head, but with the bones, with the muscles, with the joints, with the blood, with the lungs, and with the air that circulates through the lungs. Suzuki Roshi put great emphasis on physical posture. He reminded his students to watch their posture when they were studying, eating, or driving a car. He often told his students that the most important thing in taking the *zazen* posture was to keep their spines straight.

I once read about an interesting psychological study conducted at the University of Kansas in which it was demonstrated that subjects who sat in an erect posture were more encouraged to talk about themselves than when they sat in comfortable reclining postures. It was speculated that people might feel more vulnerable and ill at ease in the lying-down or sitting-bent postures.

Of course, in psychiatry or psychology, as well as in zen, the goal is not just to talk about ourself but to become more aware of ourself, to see ourself as we really are. It is only after we become aware of ourself that we find it easy to talk about ourself. It is quite probable that the sitting-erect posture of *zazen* evolved in ancient times and has continued up to this day because it is the posture which is most effective in encouraging self-awareness.

The researchers in the University of Kansas study had no satisfactory explanation for the widespread use of the reclining posture in psychoanalysis, but they wondered if the use of the psychiatric couch might be the result of some special kind of patient-specialist relationship. It is my opinion that the use of the psychiatric couch may unconsciously encourage the patient to become overly dependent upon the psychiatrist. In the posture of *zazen* one sits erect, without leaning upon anything or anyone. From the first day of zen practice, zen students, unlike psychiatric patients, are encouraged by the posture of *zazen* to become self-supporting.

Sometimes the cross-legged posture of *zazen* is recommended because it is the most stable and balanced position to maintain over long periods of meditation. If this were the only reason to cross the legs while meditating, anyone who did not intend to spend some time in a zen monastery or zen temple might be tempted to forego the discomfort of the lotus posture. But it is not just for its physical stability that the cross-legged posture is assumed. It is for its self-illuminating power as well. The broad base of the cross-legged position internalizes the foundation of Zen Buddhism.

When a person sits in the full lotus position, his left foot is on his right thigh and his right foot is on his left thigh. Suzuki Roshi pointed out that "When we cross our legs like this, even though we have a right leg and a left leg, they have become one. The position expresses the oneness of duality: not two, and not one." Suzuki Roshi said that the teaching of "not two, and not one" is the most important teaching of Buddhism. It is also one of the most difficult of the Buddhist teachings to realize, not just in the head, but in the deepest marrow of our bones. The cross-legged *mudra* of *zazen* reaches the whole heart-body-mind in a way that makes the truth of Buddhism not just secondhand information but firsthand experience.

Those who experience great pain while sitting in the cross-legged posture have, to some extent, an advantage over those who, from the first, find the posture quite comfortable. It may take longer for those who find the posture easy to realize the guts of zen.

In *zazen* we learn to reevaluate our attitude toward pain. Norman Cousins once pointed out that Americans are probably the most ignorant people on the face of the earth when it comes to the subject of physical pain. Most of us have been conditioned to believe that all pain is evil. But this is not the case. Many forms of pain are natural and normal. The important thing in understanding physical pain is to know that it increases in intensity with fear or resistance. As long as we can accept the painful legs or the sore back of *zazen* as healthy and normal kinds of pain, we will not add the extra complication of fear or resistance to our original feeling. As our ability to concentrate improves, and our dualistic habit of labeling experience as pleasant or unpleasant falls away, the physical pain of *zazen* will become less of a problem to us.

We must remember, however, that the purpose of *zazen*

is not to train spiritual athletes but to express our original nature. We should not try to force ourselves or punish ourselves with the physical posture of *zazen*. Sometimes I think that *zazen* is like toilet training. Suzuki Roshi had a very optimistic and relaxed attitude toward the habit of *zazen*. Like a good parent, he did not try to force his students before they were ready, or to make them feel ashamed if they were not able to sit in the cross-legged position for long periods without moving. The harmful effects of forced toilet training are well documented in psychological literature. I am afraid that the harmful effects of overzealous zen training have had less attention. A child who picks up good toilet habits early in life moves his bowels naturally. A zen student who picks up good zen habits early in his practice moves his mind naturally.

Suzuki Roshi occasionally made suggestions, but it was up to the student to decide for himself if he wanted to accept the suggestions or not. And Suzuki Roshi usually watched his students for some time before he began to suggest any changes. The first correction Suzuki Roshi made on my posture happened six months after I had been practicing *zazen* under his supervision. At that time Roshi pushed in my back at the waist to form a more natural curve. This small correction made a deep impression upon me.

Roshi told me that long experience had taught him that it was a waste of time to go around continually correcting the posture of zen students. A change in posture, to be effective, had to be timed to correspond with an inner ripeness. Otherwise, the correction would only result in a temporary change. Roshi let me work out the problem of my legs by myself. He never criticized me for moving in the middle of a period of *zazen*. A half-period of *zazen* done in half-lotus position hits the mark when it is done wholeheartedly. A full period of *zazen* done in full lotus posture misses the mark if it is done halfheartedly.

My own experience, though limited, has taught me that it is a waste of time to try to encourage close friends and relations to take up the practice of *zazen*. Jack has never been moved to sit in the cross-legged posture of *zazen*. I tell him that as long as *I* practice *zazen*, I am sitting for

oth of us. But if I should die first, then *he* will have to
practice *zazen* for both of us.

A zen student should take the same kind of care of his
posture as a *bonsai* master takes in shaping one of his
rees. Since each tree has its own unique physical form, a
onsai master will study the specimen for a long time
before he begins to prune or train it. And he will prune
he tree little by little. It takes many years to bring out the
natural beauty of each individual tree. We should not be
n too great a hurry to force ourselves into some preconceived mold. Little by little we should make an ad-
ustment here, or an improvement there, but we should
not expect to achieve everything in the first year or two of
practice.

If, after a reasonable trial period, you find that you are
not able to accept the cross-legged posture, then you can
at least accept the fact that you can't accept it and try to
find a posture that is more appropriate for your particular
physical-mental build. You might try a kneeling posture
with, or without, a cushion between the legs and buttocks. Some people prefer the Burmese position in which
he legs are folded but not crossed. And, of course, one
can meditate in a straight chair, sitting erect and not
leaning against the back.

A regular program of simple *yoga* exercises can often be
of help. Gautama Buddha built his Middle Way upon a
firm foundation of *yoga* training. There are many good
books on safe and simple *yoga* postures which have been
written for Westerners. I have discovered that fifteen or
twenty minutes of simple *yoga* exercises before *zazen* is a
good preparation for the mental-physical posture of *zazen*.
Every once in a while it is worth the effort to try again a
posture which you once thought was impossible. Often
changes in life-style, environment, or livelihood can ease
tensions in the body enough to permit a posture which
was once believed to be too difficult for you.

IV

Small Details

Day after day of fog and high clouds. Typical summer weather on the coast of Big Sur. Everything inside and outside looks drab: gray sky, gray ocean, gray mind. My *zazen* feels gray, and my writing reads gray.

Around noon everything begins to brighten a little. By one o'clock I can see patches of brilliant blue through the clouds. By one-thirty the fog has burned completely away, and the world, as far as I can see, shines and shimmers with psychedelic colors.

I walk slowly up the long driveway to the mailbox, filling my lungs with the incense of sage and wild mint. The weeds and grasses and wild flowers covering the banks form an intricate, interwoven pattern of delicate lines and colors. I stop and stare at a natural *mandala* (meditation picture). Faded blue morning glories are intertwined around tall white-headed yarrow; golden bush monkeys hide in the wild oats; yellow poppies cluster around a clump of purple lupine. And here, on a dry ledge, is a wild strawberry plant with a dandelion above it and a dandelion below it. I pick a tiny red strawberry and eat it. How sweet it tastes!

At first glance the *mudra* of *zazen* appears to be rather rigid and inflexible. Sometimes beginners make the mistake of trying too hard to sit like a rock. Their posture is stiff and insensitive. The physical posture of *zazen* is made up of skin, flesh, and bones. And the inner heart-mind of zen reflects the whole range of physical processes. To understand the zen mind, you must pay attention to the zen body. As Suzuki Roshi often said, the most important thing is to keep your spine straight. Keeping your spine straight is the best way to keep your head straight. But this doesn't mean straight like a dead board. It means straight like a living redwood tree.

In the posture of *zazen* the back of the head is pushed up, as if it were holding up the sky. The chin is pulled in. With the head in this position, you can feel your backbone stretching and the muscles that support the back getting a chance to strengthen themselves. When your chin is raised, you may notice the difference in the muscles that support the backbone, especially in the area of the neck. When the chin is pulled in, the backbone is strengthened. Military men understand the intimate relationship between physical posture and mental attitude.

For good physical and mental health it is very important that the spine and the nerves that are closely related to it are given as much freedom as possible, as well as the greatest muscular support. As we grow older the muscles that support our backbone grow weaker, and a deliberate effort must be made to hold ourselves erect. It is very sad to see the posture of so many young Americans today who have the mistaken idea that the way to be in tune or in harmony with nature is to let nature take its course. By the time they are twenty-five or thirty years old, many of them have such rounded shoulders and poor posture that their nature begins to look more like an animal than a human being.

There is a story about an old woman who, when she was asked the secret of her good nature and long life, replied, "When I sits I sits loose, an' I sheds all my troubles jes' like an old dress." This is a fine attitude for occasional moments of the day. We all need to know how to relax. But many young people carry the relaxed attitude to extremes. They sit loose; they stand loose; they think loose; and they live loose. And gravity takes advantage of their looseness to bend them down to a premature old age. In the practice of *zazen* we give our attention to sitting tall. Instead of just letting nature take care of us, we enter into partnership with nature. We put our mind, as well as our body, into growing in the direction of our full stature as human beings.

In the posture of *zazen* the shoulders are relaxed. This may require some special attention. Many of us have a tendency to hold our shoulders rather tensely. When the shoulders are tensed, the head begins to sink down into a hollow between the shoulders. This is a fearful position, a cramped position. With the shoulders relaxed, the chest is allowed more room to expand. The body begins to fill up its allotted space, and there is enough room to breathe deeply and live fully.

Suzuki Roshi explained the position of the hands this way: "Your hands should form the 'cosmic *mudra*.' If you put your left hand on top of your right, middle joints of your middle fingers together, and touch your thumbs lightly together (as if you held a piece of paper between them), your hands will make a beautiful oval. You should keep this universal *mudra* with great care, as if you were holding something very precious in your hand." Suzuki Roshi could tell a great deal about a student's mental condition just by looking at the hand *mudra* of the student.

Zen masters never explain everything to their students. Suzuki Roshi never corrected my hand *mudra*, and it was only recently that I realized that I tended to allow my cosmic *mudra* to tilt. Instead of taking care to see that fingers and palms were parallel to the floor (which required a deliberate effort), I had allowed myself a more natural and comfortable position in which the fingers and palms tilted at about a forty-five-degree angle from the floor. The *mudra* is the message. It told me that I had been allowing something precious to escape from my hands and my awareness. Any correction in our body posture is bound to have its effect upon our mental or spiritual posture.

When Suzuki Roshi explained the position of the arms, he said: "Your hands should be held against your body, with your thumbs at about the height of your navel." In Hindu and Buddhist meditation, the center of the body and mind resides properly and naturally in the center of the lower abdomen, in the *hara*, or—as Americans call it—the guts. When our mind is located in our head, we tend to be too intellectual; when our mind is located in the upper part of our body, we tend to be too emotional. In both instances we are top-heavy. When the cosmic *mudra* of the hands is held at the center of our body-mind, it helps us resume our original nature. From this center our mind can pervade the whole body, and the whole body can pervade the mind. Suzuki Roshi continued, on the subject of the arms: "Hold your arms freely and easily, and slightly away from your body, as if you held an egg under each arm without breaking it."

I confess that at this point I am puzzled. I wish I had discussed the eggs with my master while he was still alive. I always just imagined what it would feel like to hold an egg under each armpit and didn't give it any more thought. But now this doesn't satisfy me. Why eggs? Did zen monks in the old days actually sit in *zazen* with eggs under their armpits to keep themselves alert?

This morning I got a carton of eggs out of the cooler, spread a large bath towel on the floor, and set my meditation cushion on the towel. Then I sat down on the cushion in the *zazen mudra* and put one egg under my right armpit. (The towel was protection in case my experiment failed.) So far, so good! Getting the second egg under the left armpit was more difficult. But I found it *could* be done. And it *was* possible to sit in the *zazen mudra* holding the eggs gently under the armpits. Since the eggs were cold, I was very aware of them, but I imagine that as the eggs reached body temperature, awareness of them would begin to fade. Then the exercise would become more difficult. I didn't try a whole period of *zazen*. I was more interested to see if I could remove the eggs without breaking them. It was tricky, but it *could* be done. So now I know that even if zen monks in ancient times didn't sit with eggs under their armpits, it might be an interesting exercise for contemporary zen students to try once in a while. An old hen may be able to teach us something about zen.

In the posture of *zazen* the head is in perfect balance. The nose is in line with the navel, and the ears are in line with the shoulders. The mouth is closed, and the teeth touch lightly. The tongue rests on the upper palate, the tip lightly touching the back of the teeth. The eyes are open and focused at a comfortable position about three feet ahead. But the eyes are not really focused on anything. They see but do not actively look.

The position of the eyes is interesting. In some forms of meditation, other than zen, the eyes are closed. But closing the eyes encourages sleepiness, daydreaming, and sometimes hallucinations. Zen meditation is not a withdrawal from the outer world and a focusing on the inner world. It is awareness of both outer and inner worlds. For most of us, sight is the most dominant sense, so the position of the eyes may affect the position of all the other senses. When the eyes find their proper position in *zazen*, the other senses will tend to find their proper positions.

When Dogen Zenji, one of the great Japanese zen patriarchs, returned to Japan from his zen studies in China, he was asked what new or important teaching he had brought back to Japan from China. He said, "The eyes are placed horizontally, and the nose is placed perpendicular." This seems very obvious. But because it seems obvious we should give it more attention. Dogen Zenji's horizontal eyes may be a way of expressing the power of the eyes to see things as they are. To see true. If our eyes are level, our whole body and mind will tend to be level, and we may be in a better position to see the true way even in the darkness of our ignorance.

Of course, Dogen's statement that "the eyes are horizontal and the nose is perpendicular" does not apply only to the physical posture of *zazen*. It is another way of expressing Gautama Buddha's statement (recorded in the *Diamond Sutra*): "Through enlightenment I acquired nothing." If we become attached to the literal explanation of Dogen Zenji's statement that "the eyes are placed horizontally, and the nose is placed perpendicular," we put ourselves in the position of some eccentric zen masters who died and were buried in the *zazen* posture. Gautama Buddha expressed the real position of Zen Buddhism when he passed into *nirvana* in the normal lying-down position—with the eyes perpendicular and the nose horizontal. (Dying in the cross-legged posture is more appropriate in Tibetan Buddhism, which puts emphasis on the supernatural and is in keeping with the unusual, lofty environment of that part of the world.)

Dogen's message, like Buddha's, was that zen is nothing special, and yet this does not mean that this nothing special should be ignored or taken for granted. Everything, no matter how trivial or ordinary, should be given our fullest attention and consideration. When we give the ordinary details of our life our fullest attention, we realize that everything is truly extraordinary and wonderfully exciting in this world of ours. Nothing is unimportant.

Some attention should be given to becoming more aware of the muscles of the body. Quite often we pick up facial and body expressions from our parents and early associates that we carry with us throughout our lives. In one sense these facial and body expressions are a reflection of our unconscious attitude, and in another sense they constantly reinforce old attitudes even after we have consciously abandoned them. Allowing our tense muscles to relax during the practice of *zazen* is a way of deconditioning our body and mind from acquired habits and acquired attitudes—at the conscious as well as the unconscious levels. Do you tend to furrow your brows? Allowing the muscles of your forehead to relax may help you let go of your unconscious habit of worrying. Do you tend to clench your teeth? Allowing the muscles of the jaws to relax may relieve your unconscious tendency to hang onto things for dear life. I have a tendency to raise my eyebrows. This reminds me that, even though I consciously consider myself liberated from my puritanical heritage, there is still a puritanical tendency at work in my unconscious mind. I also suffer occasionally from a pain in the neck, which is something *I* give myself. It reminds me of the self-defeating power of my stubborn ego.

Taking care of the physical *mudra* of *zazen* will keep the beginning zen student busy for several months or more. As long as a zen student gives his physical posture full attention, there will be no great rush to burden himself with additional concentration exercises. As each period of *zazen* progresses a zen student will find that, sooner or later, his mind will begin to wander, and he will lose touch with the full reality of his posture. When this happens, his chin may begin to raise, his back may begin to sag, his eyelids may begin to droop, his hand *mudra* may begin to tilt, or his thumbs may begin to fall apart. So it is necessary for every zen student to make a constantly renewed effort to bring his attention back to the small details of posture and to make minor corrections where needed.

Even advanced students of meditation must make an effort to check the small details of their posture at regular intervals. Just because the body learns, in time, to take care of the physical posture of *zazen* without constant attention, this doesn't mean it won't need an adjustment now and then. Just this morning I realized that I was holding my hand *mudra* an inch or two below its proper position. And I also realized that I had allowed this condition to go undetected for several months. An inch or two doesn't seem to be very important, but it is like the mote Jesus spoke about in our eye. When projected on the outside world, the mote in our eye becomes the beam in our neighbor's eye. Allowing the cosmic *mudra* to settle in the region of the sexual organs lowers the point of balance below the natural center of our original nature. It may affect the whole balance of our outlook.

So taking care of the physical and mental posture of *zazen* is taking care that the skin is kept sensitive, the muscles are kept relaxed and responsive, the joints are kept flexible, the blood is kept flowing, the bones are kept strong, the body is kept well balanced, and the mind is allowed to fill the body completely.

V

Thinking

In the middle of typing over a paragraph for the third time (but not the last), I hear the soft trickling nesting call of a canyon wren. Whenever I hear the song of this shy bird, it takes me back to Tassajara. Once again I find myself sitting on my round black cushion in the *zendo*, surrounded by black-robed monks. Through the open windows I can hear the murmur of Tassajara Creek, and nearby the sounds of the kitchen crew making breakfast. It's almost the end of the second period of *zazen*, when, from the top of the *zendo* roof, the canyon wren pours out a shower of pure liquid notes that splash over sleepy bald heads and wake everyone up to the wonder of this fantastic world of ours. Though I've never heard them, I'm sure that the songs of the nightingale or the *alavinka* (a mythical Indian bird) do not compare in beauty with the song of the shy canyon wren.

Quietly I move across the room and out the open door to see if I can catch a glimpse of the bird. I don't have long to wait. The wren calls again, softly, a shimmering waterfall of crystal-clear notes. I trace the call to the source under the wooden steps that lead from the kitchen patio up to the driveway above the house. The wren must have built a nest right here under the steps. What a good omen!

The sound of the kettle of water simmering on the stove calls me to the kitchen.

"I hear you, kettle. You, too, have a beautiful song. You, too, preach the *dharma* that can never be put into words." I make myself a cup of coffee and take it outside.

I sit down on the old wooden bench in the little kitchen patio. The begonias look dry. The chrysanthemums need pinching back, and the dead nasturtium blossoms should be picked. When I'm finished with my coffee, I'll put away my typewriter for the day. My unfinished paragraph will polish itself naturally while I water the plants and pull some weeds in the garden.

After a zen student has fully settled his body into the position of *zazen*, he is in a position to settle his mind. Our thinking mind is used to keeping itself very busy. It prides itself on its ability to work day and night. But actually, our thinking mind has a problem. It doesn't know how to relax. The practice of *zazen* is a time when we allow the thinking mind to come to a well-needed rest. Only after the thinking mind has settled down in the center of existence will we be in a position to resume our original nature.

A monk asked a zen master, "What is zen?" The master replied, "I eat when I eat, and I sleep when I sleep." The monk asked, "Isn't that what everyone does?" The master replied, "Not at all. When most people eat they think of other things; and when most people sleep they dream of other places." The practice of *zazen* encourages a person to put his whole body and mind where it belongs, in the actual physical reality of the moment, rather than allowing the mind to drift away into some other time or place. When the mind is allowed to wander away from the body, even for just a few minutes or just a few inches, the body and mind are split, and this division, if prolonged, tends to cause internal conflicts. When internal conflicts are projected outside, external problems are created.

Before we begin the practice of *zazen*, it is almost impossible to realize that the biggest source of human suffering could be such a simple thing as the habit of letting our mind wander away from its home. The conflict, suffering, and turmoil caused by the division of mind and body add confusion to the problem. Secondary habits, such as over-indulgence in alcohol, drugs, TV, work, or religious fanaticism, are some of the extras which are often added to the original discontent created by the split between mind and body. But underneath all the confusion of the surface symptoms lies the basic and undetected problem, the mischief created by the thinking faculty.

Before we begin the practice of *zazen*, we are not aware of how carried away we are most of the time by our thinking. The old saying which goes: "A man takes the first drink; a drink takes the second drink; and the third drink takes the man," is just as true with thinking as it is with drinking. The first thought leads to another, and then another, and another, and before we realize it, several hours have disappeared from our lives. Whenever our body is doing one thing and our mind is somewhere else, we are actually living some imaginary life, and we have missed living that much of our actual life. This is why we feel cheated. Actually, we cheat ourselves. Living in some imaginary life can be very intoxicating. It often seems more interesting than our real life. But sooner or later the imaginary life wears off, and then we find ourselves back in the same old reality again, and we have added something extra to it—a splitting headache.

When we live completely in the actual reality of our own life, with our whole body and mind, it is like drinking milk. Drinking milk may seem very ordinary compared to drinking alcohol. To an alcoholic, milk may even taste like medicine. But the aftereffects of drinking milk are very beneficial. In the same way, when we live completely in the full reality of our own life, the aftereffects of this way of living leave us with a sense of physical and mental well-being. So the practice of *zazen* is as natural and as ordinary as drinking milk. *Zazen* may be more like drinking homogenized milk. For *zazen* unites or homogenizes all the senses into a harmonious blend that enables our mind to digest all experiences evenly and efficiently.

When we begin the practice of *zazen*, it is like joining Thinkers Anonymous. Before we take up the practice of *zazen*, we first have to admit to ourselves that we have become mentally confused. Our life may have presented us with a natural *koan*, a problem which we are not able to solve by thinking. At this time it is almost impossible to see that it is thinking itself that is really our problem. Western civilization has conditioned us to put values on different kinds of thinking. Some kinds of thinking are considered profitable and other kinds harmful. Wishful thinking, fantasizing, daydreaming, and imagining are usually looked upon as inferior forms of thinking; while planning, remembering, reasoning, judging, comparing, discriminating, reflecting, selecting, or contemplating are believed to be higher modes of thought.

In the Western countries overindulgence in daydreaming is recognized, by most people, to be unhealthy. We say that a person who fantasizes a great deal of the time loses touch with reality. But it is not easy for most Westerners to appreciate the fact that anyone who overindulges in reasoning, planning, or any other of the "higher" forms of thought is also liable to lose touch with reality. Reality is beyond thinking. Reality cannot be touched directly by thought. But only when reality *is* touched directly, not only with the body but with the mind as well, is life fully realized. The mind that can touch reality directly is the original mind before it is divided by thought. The original mind in its unconditioned state is clear, empty, and alert. It is pure awareness without any distortions produced by thinking.

After we begin the practice of *zazen* we may make the mistake of trying to eliminate all our thoughts. But Thinkers Anonymous, unlike Alcoholics Anonymous, does not recommend total abstinence. Overthinking is more like overeating. It is possible to abstain totally from drinking alcohol and still live a perfectly normal life. But we must eat. And as long as we live in this world, thoughts will appear in our mind. It is only when we have allowed ourselves to be carried away by our thinking process that we may find it necessary to follow a mental exercise program for a while to get our mind back in shape. But here, too, we must be careful. If we go on a crash diet, or try to starve our mind, it will only work for a while; but sooner or later we will go back to gorging ourselves again. It isn't the thoughts themselves that create problems, but the *attachment* to those thoughts.

The way we handle the situation is just to let the thoughts come in and let them go out without getting attached to their delicious or unpleasant flavors. Whenever we discover that our mind is wandering, we learn to lead it gently back home to the present environment. In this way our mind will digest all the thoughts that appear in it, and gradually they'll decrease. When the occasion arises in which it is appropriate to put our whole body and mind into thinking (working on some problem which can be solved by thinking), we will find our thinking faculty much improved in performance. Of course, it takes some time before we are able to recognize the kind of problem that can be solved by thinking, and the kind of problem that can only be confused by thinking.

Shakespeare said, "There is nothing either good or bad but thinking makes it so." Because our culture has overemphasized the value of thinking, considering it good, we must be careful not to overreact and jump to the conclusion that thinking is bad. Thinking is neither good nor bad. It is a function of human life, like eating. If we are attached to eating, our body suffers physically. If we are attached to thinking, our body suffers mentally. Attachment is created when we think something is either good or bad.

Zazen is sometimes called mind-fasting. There is some resemblance between physical fasting and mind-fasting. Although I have not fasted physically for a long period of time, I understand that in the process of fasting there is a period of several days in which a false hunger is experienced. Then a period of a week or two (or in some cases longer) follows in which no hunger is felt. Finally true hunger is experienced. Our ordinary mental activity may be like false hunger. Right thinking, or true thinking, may be like true hunger. The difference between false thinking and true thinking can be appreciated in the experience of mental fasting or *zazen*.

If we can imagine Buddha's Noble Eightfold Path as forming a circle, the step of right thought is next to the step of right meditation. When we understand right meditation, we are able to take one more step and return to thinking, not false thinking, but true thinking. Right thinking is concentrated, clear, penetrating, and free from selfish desires. This kind of thinking does not carry us away from ourself. It leads us deeper into our original nature—into harmony with the whole zen environment.

VI

Counting to Ten

E very morning, after I've made the beds, washed the breakfast dishes, dusted, and vacuumed, I fill the two bird feeders on the front deck with birdseed. As soon as I leave, the black and blue Steller's jays, which have been keeping a lookout from the tall pines to the south, swoop in and begin jostling each other for the best perches on the feeders. The meal is a lively one, accompanied by loud squawks and flapping wings. Seeds and feathers fly in every direction.

Steller's jays are rather lowbrow creatures. Loudmouthed and macho. They are clever imitators of other birds' calls, especially the scream of the red-tailed hawk. Jays chase away most of the well-mannered birds in their territory. But not all of them.

Drawn by the cries of the Steller's jays, an aristocratic family of redheaded acorn woodpeckers are approaching the deck. All of the jays depart abruptly—all, that is, except one young and inexperienced bird. A sharp peck from the beak of the eldest woodpecker sends the young jay crying to his mama.

With their red-capped heads and their black and white wings, the woodpeckers are beautiful, and they know it. They are well mannered in their habits. Each finds a place around the feeder, and none, not even the youngest, throws food on the floor. When all are finished with their meal, they leave together.

The jays straggle back to the bird feeders by ones and twos. The young ones pick at their food and then fly off. The older jays stay longer, but they do more squawking than eating. By the time the last one leaves, the porch is a mess.

If our thinking mind is very rebellious, we may give it an exercise during *zazen* to keep it out of mischief until it begins to settle down. The first exercise often given to zen students is the one of counting their breaths from one to ten. Sometimes the student is instructed to count the inhalation of the breath as one, and the exhalation as two, and so on until he reaches ten. Then the process is started all over again. Sometimes only the inhalations are counted. Sometimes only the exhalations (which is the method recommended by Suzuki Roshi). But all students are instructed to count to ten and no further.

Quite often, especially at first, a zen student is not able to reach number ten before his mind begins to wander off on some train of thought. When this happens, no matter how often, the student should be careful not to be critical of his performance or to feel that he has failed in any way. As soon as he discovers the fact that he is not counting his breaths but is daydreaming, he should simply take note of the fact and return to the exercise of counting his breaths beginning with number one.

The practice of *zazen* is not setting up some goal, such as counting to ten perfectly over and over for a whole period of *zazen*. In the practice of *zazen* we are not in competition with anyone, not even ourselves. Some days it will be very easy to concentrate, and other days it will be very difficult. But as long as we continue the practice of *zazen*, through settled mental weather and unsettled, the practice will carry us to the heart of our original nature. Each time we return from our mind-wandering, we return to the center of our zen practice, the center of our zen environment.

Very often the exercise of counting breaths from one to ten is considered a preliminary zen training exercise, a preparation for the real practice of *zazen*. But Suzuki Roshi did not consider it so. In order to emphasize this point he once had his students at Zenshinji Monastery concentrate for a whole *sesshin* (a period of intensive meditation lasting a week) on nothing but the exercise of counting breaths. All students, advanced and beginning—and even the

Roshi—practiced counting breaths from one to ten. Suzuki Roshi said that those students who wished could keep this practice for the rest of their lives. Considered from the viewpoint of true zen practice, the exercise of counting breaths is no less enlightening than the more advanced practice of *shikan-taza*, or themeless meditation.

Counting breaths from one to ten, when done with wholehearted attention, can become a kind of *mantra*. *Mantra* is a Sanskrit word for a mystical or magical word or formula which is spoken over and over, out loud or silently, in order to awaken original nature. The Hindu sound of *Aum* is used as a *mantra* to help bring the worshiper to the realization of his original nature, which the Hindu calls *Brahman*. The Lord's Prayer is used by Christians to bring them closer to their original nature, which they call God. In the Buddhist sect of Jodo Shin the *mantra* "*Namu Amida Butsu*" (Adoration to the Buddha Amida) is believed by all its devotees to be the most effective method of crossing over from the shore of ignorance and suffering to the shore of original nature, which the Shin Buddhist calls the Pure Land of Amida Buddha. The Zen Buddhist *koan* of *Mu* has the power of a *mantra*.

Actually, the magic power of the *mantra*, like the magic power of the *mudra*, is not something supernatural. When the meditating student fills his mind day and night with nothing but the sound and thought of his *mantra*, he interrupts the habitual flow of self-centered thoughts that normally disturb and distort his pure awareness. The *mantra* may be like an erase head on a tape recorder. The perfect erase head is *shikan-taza*, or themeless meditation. *Shikan-taza* allows the self-centered thoughts to flow uninterruptedly through the mind but erases the *attachment* to the thoughts. *Shikan-taza* requires a good balance of mind and body to be effective, and so it is seldom given to beginning zen students.

The devotional *mantras* such as the Lord's Prayer and the Amida Buddha prayer are, perhaps, the easiest for religiously minded people to accept wholeheartedly. But this type of *mantra* leaves a film of religious attachment covering pure awareness. Zen Buddhist *koans* leave no trace of holiness, but they require the regular adjustment of a zen master over a long period of time to erase all traces of intellectual activity. The exercise of counting breaths from one to ten is perhaps the safest *mantra* for a student who must practice without a zen teacher. He is not apt to get caught by the exercise in some religious hallucination and is not apt to get trapped in a dualistic impasse. Counting over and over from one to ten may seem very dull and mechanical, but it can become a very enlightening practice.

In traditional zen training a student practices with a zen master for at least ten years before he begins to teach others. Before I began the practice of *zazen* I thought that this meant that it took at least ten years before a student could become an expert of zen. I thought that acquiring zen training was something like acquiring the skills of a musician or a surgeon. But I discovered that zen is not as simple as this. After I began the practice of *zazen* and learned the exercise of counting breaths, I thought that becoming an adept of zen was something like the ability to return to the unspoiled mind of a child. But zen is not as simple as this either. The simplicity of zen is beyond the usual categories of beginner or expert.

Ten is a combination of two symbols, the symbol for number one (which represents something) and the symbol for zero (which represents nothing). It is important to remember that in the history of mankind the discovery of the numbers representing something came long before the discovery of the symbol which represents nothing. One of my zen teachers, Kobun Chino Roshi, said once that zen is to life what the zero is to mathematics. He said the discovery of the zero made mathematics possible. He pointed out that, in one sense, there is no value to zen, just as there is no value to the zero. But just as the zero expands the possibilities of mathematics immeasurably, so zen infinitely expands the possibilities of our life.

When we begin the exercise of counting our breaths in *zazen*, we begin with number one. We do not begin with zero. It is easier for us to understand something than to understand nothing. It is easier to meditate on a theme than on no theme. It is only when we arrive at the number ten, or completion, that we become aware of the zero, or nothing. Actually, when we arrive at number ten, we have already gone back to number one, *and* to the realm that includes all numbers. Number ten is the number which represents both the beginning (one, or the beginner's mind) and the end (ten, or the expert's mind), as well as everything in between, *plus* zero (nothing or original mind). This "nothing" is sometimes called Vast Emptiness or *sunyata* or *nirvana* or Buddha-nature, which are all different names for the same nothingness.

Suzuki Roshi said once that he had discovered "that it is necessary, absolutely necessary, to believe in nothing. That is, we have to believe in something which has no form and no color—something which exists before all forms and colors appear." Something like the zero which by itself has no value, but when combined with something else has infinite value. Mathematics begins with the discovery of the nothingness of the zero. Our life begins with the discovery of the nothingness of zen. When zen is completely united with our life, our old self-imposed limitations fall away. We become aware of our total environment. So ten years of zen practice, or counting to ten in *zazen*, is the realization (making real) of something which is nothing. It is the discovery of our original nature.

Recently I have discovered that it is necessary, absolutely necessary (for survival), to acquire the habit of going back to the beginning. This is one of the most important habits we can acquire from the enlightening zen practice of counting breaths from one to ten. When we lose count during this zen exercise, we are instructed to return to the beginning and start over. And if we reach the goal, we are also instructed to return to the beginning and start over. Counting practice is one of the basic activities of our original mind. There is a big difference between the activity of our original mind and the usual activity of our thinking mind. When our thinking mind loses count, it gets distracted and wanders way off the track. And if our thinking mind arrives at its goal, it wants to continue on and on, counting to a hundred, or a thousand, or a million. Our thinking mind loves to complicate and refine something that is already complete. Our thinking mind always tries to improve upon the perfect practice of our original nature.

Applied to everyday life, counting practice means that

when we find that we have lost our touch, when our work has become confusing or complicated, or if we find ourselves stuck in a rut, we should not try to go forward (as the thinking mind always wants to do), but we should go back to the beginning and start over again, concentrating on our beginning practice of *zazen*. And if we find that we have reached our goal, that our life has become complete, clear, uncomplicated, and is going forward successfully, then we should *still* return to the beginning and start over. If we continue on and on, up the ladder of success, our thinking mind will complicate and confuse our success.

There are two excellent ways to go back to the beginning after having reached a goal. One is to become a teacher of beginning students. And the other is to become a student in a new field. Both of these positions encourage us to return to our beginner's mind. When Zen Buddhism reaches a certain point of refinement in a person or a culture, it is moved by its original nature on to a new person or a new culture. Japanese Zen Buddhism is very refined today. It has been polished to perfection. So in order to survive, it has moved West to a new culture. We, in America today, live in a most important and exciting period of Zen Buddhism, a period that can completely revolutionize not only the American zen spirit but also the Japanese zen spirit.

But the zen practice of returning to the beginning is not limited to Zen Buddhism. This practice is the key to survival of all religions. And this practice is important in all activities of our life—in politics, art, economics, science, business, marriage, child rearing, teaching, or in whatever other fields we might be engaged.

Often we hear the mass-produced thinking mind proclaiming: *"It is impossible to go back!"* And because we have lost touch with the basic practice of our original nature, we go along with the argument and allow our lives to become more and more complicated, more and more restricted, and more and more carried away by gadgets and frivolous attachments. This is why it is necessary, absolutely necessary—not only for personal survival, but for the survival of our culture and for the survival of the human race—to put more emphasis on the basic zen practice of counting our breaths from one to ten.

VII

Life and Breath

For several weeks I have been holding my breath, putting off beginning this chapter. I've polished some earlier chapters, written first drafts of later chapters, accomplished enough to satisfy my skin-deep request. But I have not even tickled the interest of my inmost request. Holding the breath is clinging to the known. It is fear of letting go and plunging into the unknown. There is something in the realm of breathing that I can't quite grasp. It is not so difficult to express the basic posture of the zen environment. Posture is something relatively solid and easy to grasp. But the basic activity of the zen environment, the rhythm of breathing, is in constant flux. Holding it, it eludes me. Here, in the acitvity of the breathing process, we finally approach the original nature of zen.

Fearing the unknown, we cling to the known. Fearing the unknown, we often label it impossible. After Shakyamuni's awakenment under his own self-illuminating power, Buddha realized that it would be impossible to express this kind of knowledge to anyone who had not experienced it for himself. And if some other person *had* experienced what Buddha had experienced, there was nothing Buddha could add, or take away, from that other person's own experience. And so Buddha decided that he would keep his enlightenment to himself and not waste his time trying to help anyone else attain enlightenment.

But on deeper and more compassionate reflection, Buddha was moved to try to do the impossible.

Suzuki Roshi once said, "To think, 'Because it is possible we will do it,' is not Buddhism. Even though it is impossible, we have to do it because our true nature wants us to." The great enlightenment Buddha experienced under the Bodhi Tree was just one of Buddha's great enlightenments. The decision to try to express what he had experienced, even though it was impossible, was another great enlightenment. Without the second enlightenment, the first enlightenment would have soon turned into his old hometown. There is nothing deader than yesterday's enlightenment. Buddha's decision to teach opened up to him the path by which he could deepen and extend a life of continuously unfolding enlightenment.

In order to detach myself from my old hometown, I move my typewriter from the big redwood table that I have been using as a desk to the floor in front of the sliding window-door that divides the living room from the outside deck. Sitting on the floor in front of my typewriter, with my legs crossed, I am in the posture of even-though-it-is-impossible-I'll-do-it. The door is opened to new possibilities. I relax and allow myself to be at home in my environment. The woodpeckers and the blue jays have just finished their breakfast at the bird feeder. A chipmunk is scampering around the deck between the potted plants, gathering up the seed offerings the birds have left him. A little later in the morning the gray squirrels will drop by on their rounds. An adventurous hummingbird, noticing that both front door and deck doors are open, takes a zooming shortcut through the living room, surprising me so that my head is cleared of some of its old attachments. It is very satisfying to be so intimately related to life—to watch the wild creatures come in and go out, moving naturally and unhindered, each following its own rhythm. A wind bell tinkles. The morning mist drifts up the canyon through the tall pines and redwoods. Later on the fog will clear, and I will be able to see the great pacific ocean of unlimited possibilities.

In *Yoga*, which is the old hometown of Buddhism, the

breathing is strictly regulated. In zen, the breathing is allowed to return to its natural rhythm. There is a saying in zen: "A long breath is long, and a short breath is short." This means, rather than creating some artificial way of breathing on the one hand, or just taking our breathing for granted on the other hand, we give some attention to the basic activity of our life. Instead of counting our breaths, which is a way of concentrating our attention on our breathing, we begin to take care of our breathing. And the way to take care of our breathing is to give it our full attention; we follow our breathing. At first we will probably be following someone else's breathing. We will be following the breathing of our false self. Just as we pick up facial habits and unconscious attitudes from our parents and other childhood relationships, we also pick up habits of breathing and rhythms of living that are not truly our own.

The breathing of our false self is apt to be shallow and may not extend below the emotional level of the chest. The breathing of our original nature reaches down into the center of being, to the *hara*, to the guts. But before we try prematurely to correct our false breathing habits, we should allow ourselves to become thoroughly familiar with them. When we becomme intimate with our false rhythm of breathing and our false way of living without trying to change them, then our original nature will be awakened, and we will begin to resume it naturally.

The problem of breathing is closely connected with the problem of life and death. Because most of us cling to life (the known) and fear death (the unknown), we may tend to hold our breath. Consciously and unconsciously, breathing is associated with life. But actually, breathing is the fundamental process of life *and* death. Each complete breath is made up of an inhalation (inspiration) and an exhalation (expiration). In other words, it is one complete life and one complete death. But we tend to hold on to inspiration. To be filled with inspiration means to be filled with spirit. And yet Jesus, who had much to teach us about zen, did not say, "Blessed are the *full* in spirit"; he said, "Blessed are the *poor* in spirit, for *theirs* is the kingdom of heaven." Poverty is the fundamental aspect of almost every religious teaching. And the fundamental poverty is the poverty of spirit, the letting go of life and breath.

Only when we let go of our old breath and throw away our old life, will we be in a position to be filled with new life, new breath, and new spirit. Because of our tendency to cling to life and breath, it may be necessary to put a gentle, but firm, emphasis on the process of exhalation. We should not be afraid to experience complete expiration. It is a paradox that, even though we experience thousands of deaths each day of our lives, we still fear the idea of death. Because we concentrate on life, on inspiration, and avoid death, or expiration, we do not completely expel our period of death. And we bring a trace of death into each new life.

The way to realize fully each life and each death is to take care of our breathing, to be sure that we allow each breath to expire fully, to die completely. After it dies completely, the new breath will follow spontaneously and naturally, filling the emptiness left by the complete expiration. Paying attention to our breathing is the fundamental activity of *zazen*. When the breathing is restored to its natural rhythm and its balanced position, then every other activity will fall naturally into its own balanced rhythm. When we stop holding our breath, we stop clinging to life. We concentrate on taking care of the period of inspiration until the moment when it turns naturally into the period of expiration, and then we instantly let go of the period of inspiration and concentrate fully on the period of expiration.

Life should be life with no trace of death. Death should be death with no trace of life. When we take care of our breathing in this way, we will find that the problem of our life and breath will take care of itself. Life and breath will pervade the whole body, the whole mind, flowing through us like the tide flows back and forth through a net. And when the net of the processes, which we call our human being, disappears, the tide of our life and breath will continue to flow in and out of the whole zen environment.

VIII

Appreciating Life

"Are you awake?"

"Umhum." (I'm only half awake.)

"Hear the coyotes barking?"

"Umm. Beautiful."

"Do you feel like getting up?"

"What time is it?"

"Three-thirty. I can't sleep."

"OK. If you want to." I start to get out of bed.

Jack turns on the light. "No, you stay in bed. I'll make the coffee this morning."

I sink back gratefully and doze off to the sound of coyotes barking down in the canyon. . . .

"Here's your coffee," Jack says, putting a cup on the table beside my bed. We prop up our pillows and sit up in bed, drinking our coffee.

"I'm getting tired of living in other people's houses," Jack says.

"I know how you feel, but . . ."

"Do you mind if I dream out loud?"

"Of course not. I promise I won't interrupt you again until you're finished."

"Thanks." Jack pauses while he collects his thoughts and then says, "I know I should be grateful for being able to live here. There are thousands of people who would gladly change places with me. And I'm grateful to have a little work to do. I enjoy working. Except for people I don't respect. And it's nice to have a little money to spend on necessities. But living in someone else's house..."

I restrain my urge to interrupt.

"You know what I'd really like to do?"

"What?"

"I'd like to go up on a mountainside someplace and build myself a house. A cabin. I'd use old boards, rusty tin, rocks, anything that would make it look like a part of the mountain. I'd put a front porch on it. And if you want to get down to the knives and forks and spoons and saucers—nothing in my cabin would be the same. No dish would be alike. I would have the fanciest china-gold-painted-cup-you-could-almost-see-through for my coffee in the morning on my front porch. And I would wear my oldest clothes. And cook with wood. And I'd have kerosene lamps. And I'd have you to talk to. You'd be there.

"And I'd build myself a little workshop where I could get into some ideas that I've been thinking about for a long time. I gotta have a place of my own before I can build these things. I need a place where I can keep my tools and my materials—a place where I can work without anyone looking over my shoulder or telling me that I've gotta move next month because the place has been sold.

"And when I got tired of working outside all day building rock walls or digging in the garden, and tired of working in my shop half the night, I'd quit for a day or two and sit in the sun. I'd eat and sleep and do nothing for a while but just stare at nothing which is all around me. And then I'd go back to work again. On my own projects. On my own schedule. Work when I'm moved to work, eat when I'm moved to eat, shit when I'm moved to shit, piss when I'm moved to piss, and do nothing when I'm moved to do nothing."

There is a long silence.

"Maybe that's not just a dream," I say. "Maybe it's more like a premonition. Maybe someday you and I will be living in a cabin on the side of a mountain, and I'll remind you of your old dream. By that time you probably will be so busy working on your projects that you will have forgotten it."

"Maybe so."

There is another long silence. Jack breaks it. "Well, that's enough dreaming. We're here now, and I've got a big plumbing job to do today. How about getting your ass out of bed and making me some breakfast so I can get an early start?"

The ability to concentrate completely on something such as the posture of *zazen*, or breathing, or on some problem such as a *koan*, is a form of zen meditation, but it isn't what is meant by "right meditation" or "perfect meditation," the eighth step in Buddha's Middle Way. In the Japanese language, "right meditation" is expressed by a unique phrase: *shikan-taza*. *Shikan-taza* is usually translated "themeless meditation." Rather than concentrating on something such as a *koan*, the activity of *shikan-taza* concentrates on nothing. Sometimes *shikan-taza* is translated "just sitting."

Shikan means "right," "just it," "earnestly," "for itself," or (the translation I prefer) "for the sake of itself." *Ta* means "a complete action." The action of *ta* is one with no beginning and no end; it is an activity that is interconnected with everything in the universe: past, present, and future. *Za* means "to sit in the posture of *zazen*." One of my zen teachers, Katagiri Roshi, said that *taza* means "to sit up to the hilt." So *shikan-taza* means to sit wholeheartedly for the sake of itself. There are no future goals in *shikan-taza*. The goal (enlightenment) and the means (*zazen*) are one complete activity: *ta*.

There is a short story which illustrates something about the difference between ordinary meditation and *shikan-taza*. Once Lao-tzu, the legendary Chinese Taoist sage, was taking a journey with his attendant to a distant city. After traveling for many days, the two came to a place where they could see the city ahead. The attendant, seeing the end of the journey in sight, spurred on his horse. But Lao-tzu called the young man back, saying, "Here too it is good!" and rode steadily on.

It's not that we should never have future goals, but we should be careful not to get attached to future goals and let them carry us from the true goal. All future goals can only be tentative. The only real goal is the one which exists here and now in this time and place.

Ordinary meditation, or zazen practiced in the ordinary was, is done for the purpose of attaining something such as peace of mind or enlightenment. Perfect meditation, or shikan-taza, is done for the sake of itself. You may remember that I explained that karmic reaction is produced by action that has a motive, action that seeks a result. This is the reason ordinary zazen, which is a means to an end, creates karmic reaction. Karmic reactions are attachments to people, places, things, and ideas. Shikan-taza, however, produces no karmic reactions because it is done for the sake of itself.

One of my zen teachers, Kobun Chino Roshi, said: "Shikan-taza has a kind of slippery feeling to it. This means that it is easy to slip off from it. It's quite slippery because it relates to your everyday condition. Each sitting you have to sense it without anyone's help. There are no techniques in it. No techniques means there is no kind of measuring stick to evaluate it. There is no way of knowing what it is or what you are doing. All kinds of conceptualizations, ideas, hopes, fall off from it. They do not stay; they cannot stay in your meditation."

If someone were to ask me today, "What is shikan-taza?" I would say, "Shikan-taza is a black hole in inner space which is created when an ego collapses upon itself." Shikan-taza creates a gravitational pull so powerful that all thoughts, all feelings, and all sensations disappear into it. This may be the reason that there are no feelings of physical or spiritual joy in perfect meditation.

Sometimes shikan-taza is translated "to give up illusions and attain enlightenment." Actually, giving up illusions is enlightenment. Shikan-taza is sudden enlightenment. There is no gap between the activity of shikan-taza and the attainment of enlightenment. Whenever you sit in zazen, wholeheartedly, without any motive, you are suddenly enlightened. Whenever you sit in zazen with an aim to becoming enlightened, you are only attached to an illusion of enlightenment.

After I've said this much about shikan-taza, I must confess that I've never experienced it myself. And I must warn you that if you expect to experience it yourself you will be disappointed. There is no way you or I can experience *shikan-taza* because there is no you or I in the activity of *shikan-taza*. *Shikan-taza* is egoless meditation. That's why *shikan-taza* is called right meditation or perfect meditation. Even though it appears as if someone is meditating, *shikan-taza* is an activity that transcends the personal realm.

No zen teacher can show a student how to meditate perfectly. All a teacher can do is show a student how to meditate in the ordinary ways, suggesting some techniques such as counting breaths or concentrating on a *koan*. Perhaps the best advice a zen teacher can give to a student wishing to attain perfect meditation is the advice Katagiri Roshi once gave me. He said: "No aims; no expectations!"

Don't worry if you aren't aware of *shikan-taza* in your zen practice, even if you have been meditating for many years. It's there in the background of your meditation even when you aren't aware of it. If *shikan-taza* wasn't in the background of your meditation, you wouldn't be able to continue zen practice.

When you sit in *shikan-taza*, you will be able to appreciate the value of the perfect zen life, one lived wholeheartedly, up to the hilt, for the sake of nothing but itself. The word "appreciate" is a very interesting word which might even be used as a synonym for *shikan-taza*. Appreciate may mean: 1) to be fully aware of; 2) to increase the value of; 3) to recognize the worth of; 4) to be thankful for. The activity of *shikan-taza* helps us become more aware of our life. Becoming more aware of our life automatically increases the value of it. When the value of our life is increased, we are able to recognize the worth of it. And when we recognize the worth of our life we become thankful for it. So appreciation of our everyday life can be the means as well as the goal of *shikan-taza*.

IX

Jumping to Conclusions

Before we can live a life of *shikan-taza*, free from self-frustration and self-delusion, we must first make a deliberate and constantly renewed effort to avoid jumping to conclusions. The thinking faculty, spurred by the ego, has a tendency to rush impulsively ahead to explain every event, the instant it happens, in such a way that it fits into the dualistic framework of its own limited description of reality. When the thinking faculty jumps ahead of the intuitive wisdom of the whole body-mind (the one that extends beyond the imaginary limits of the skin-barrier), it assumes the role of leader. But the proper position of the thinking faculty, like the proper position of Lao-tzu's attendant, is riding beside or slightly behind our sage-nature. When the thinking faculty constantly jumps ahead of the intuitive wisdom of our original nature, it deludes itself into believing that *it* is leading the way. But the way is going its own way. Life is proceeding, accompanied by thought.

From the time a child enters the fascinating world of words and concepts, his original nature or Buddha-nature begins to fall dormant. By the time an adult has become fully indoctrinated into membership in the thinking race, his intuitive awareness has gone into hibernation. The practice of *zazen* reawakens the dormant levels of our original intuitive nature. When the intuitive genius of our original nature is able to observe itself in the present moment, without the constant interference of the thinking faculty's preconceived and preconditioned conclusions, the reality of the present moment is rediscovered.

Albert Einstein once told a friend, "When I asked myself how it happened that I in particular discovered the Relativity Theory, it seemed to lie in the following circumstance. The normal adult never bothers his head about space-time problems. Everything to be thought about, in his opinion, has already been done in early childhood. I, on the contrary, developed so slowly that I only began to wonder about space and time when I was already grown up. In consequence I probed deeper into the problem than an ordinary child would have done." Instead of thinking about time and space through the mental screen of an ordinary mind, Einstein was able to avoid jumping to childish conclusions and to observe things-as-they-are with his innate intuitive wisdom.

It is extremely difficult for human beings to suspend judgment and learn just to observe. A life of *shikan-taza* is a life in which the tendency of the thinking faculty to jump ahead of the whole body-mind-environment has been corrected. The practice of *zazen* allows the gears of the thinking faculty to idle. The practice of *zazen* does not attempt to stop all thinking but allows our mind to disengage itself from attachment to conclusions continually being presented to it by the ordinary thinking process.

When Shakespeare said, "Nothing is either good or bad but thinking makes it so," he was very close to expressing the essence of Zen Buddhism. The zen sage might go one step further and say, "Nothing is, or isn't, but thinking makes it so." Thinking may be said to be the doing of everything, and not thinking (not being attached to the conclusions of thinking), the undoing of everything. Dogen Zenji said that "*Zazen* is non-doing." *Zazen* is the undoing of the mischief created by attachment to the dualistic conclusions reached prematurely by the thinking faculty.

The Chinese zen master Huang-po told his disciple, "If you would spend all your time—walking, standing, sitting, or lying down—learning to halt the concept-forming activities of your own mind, you could be sure of ultimately attaining the goal. Since your strength is insufficient, you might not be able to transcend *samsara* by a single leap; but, after five or ten years, you would surely have made a good beginning and be able to make further progress spontaneously." (*Samsara*, here, means the attachment to the false conclusions of the thinking faculty.)

Learning to halt the concept-forming activities of our mind is learning to stop jumping to conclusions. This is the non-doing of *zazen*. Making further progress spontaneously is living a life of *shikan-taza*, a life freed from the self-delusion and self-frustration created by the egoistic thinking faculty. Because our thinking faculty, unlike Albert Einstein's or Hui-neng's, developed much too quickly, it may take us five or ten years of constantly renewed effort before it is able spontaneously to resume its original nature. In the meantime, if we begin to be aware of how quickly our mind tends to jump to conclusions, we can avoid getting caught in karmic consequences by not allowing ourselves to become too attached to those conclusions.

The practice of *zazen* harmonizes our mental functions with our Buddha-nature or sage-nature. Since our Buddha-nature moves on steadily, in harmony with the whole zen environment, like Lao-tzu and his attendant riding on a journey toward a distant city, harmonizing our thinking faculty with our intuitive wisdom brings it into harmony with the whole environment. It is from this harmonized viewpoint that we begin to realize that everything is Buddha-nature, everything is intuitive nature, and everything is intuitively and ecologically interconnected and interdependent. It is from this harmonized viewpoint that we begin truly to appreciate the value of our zen environment.

X

Selflessness

A covey of quails, mama, papa, and a brood of tiny little ones, appear from the brush on the side of the driveway. They are halfway across the road before they see me walking toward them. The parents signal the little ones with a warning cry, and the babies scurry to cover. The male and female keep to the center of the road about fifteen feet in front of me. Looking back at me they call, "Look at us. We're nice big fat birds. Come and catch us if you can." Knowing that their inmost request at this moment is to lure me away from their brood, I keep walking steadily up the road, pretending to follow them. Not until I am around the bend, out of sight of the place where the babies took cover, do the parents fly off into the brush. And not until they are sure that all danger is past will they go back and gather up their children.

Dogen Zenji says: "Observe how even animals and insects nurture their young, enduring various hardships in the process. The parents stand to gain nothing by their actions, even after their offspring have reached maturity. Yet, though they are only small creatures, they have deep compassion for their young. This is also the case with regard to the various Buddhas' compassion for all sentient beings."

One day Suzuki Roshi turned his back to his students, pulled his robes up over his knees, leaned over, stuck his head between his legs, and grinned at his surprised audience. Everyone laughed. To the students the zen master looked like a mischievous child. But when Suzuki Roshi announced: "This is a demonstration of your English word *understand*," the zen students could not help but laugh at themselves. A zen master will often behave in a most outrageous manner in order to help his students get better acquainted with the mischief created by the thinking process. Ninety-nine percent of the time, when we think we understand ourselves and the world, we actually stand under ourselves and look at the world with our heads stuck between our legs.

In Buddhism the idea of an unchanging and individual self, or soul, is called a topsy-turvy view. It is not easy to give up our childish attachment to the idea of a separate self. It usually takes a long period of meditation before the topsy-turvy intellectual understanding of reality is replaced by actual experiential confirmation of the true state of affairs. The illusion of a separate self begins early in life. When a child is very young, it is taught that it has a name and a separate identity from other members of the family. This is a very revolutionary discovery for a child. The ideas of "me" and "mine" become exciting tools which the child learns quickly to manipulate to its own advantage. The ordinary person solves the problem of self very early in life and never bothers to give it a second thought from then on. But Gautama Buddha took up the question of self when he was an adult, and probed the concept until all the childish fantasies had completely disappeared.

Gautama Buddha spent many years studying the philosophies of his day and searching for what his Indian teachers called his true self, or *atman*. The notion of the Hindu *atman*, as it was degraded at the time of Shakyamuni, resembled our popular notion of the Christian soul. The *atman* was thought to be personal, substantial, and eternal. Indian sages of Buddha's time believed that, by spiritual exercises, the personal *atman* could be united during life with *Brahman* (ultimate reality or great soul of the universe). Buddha was told that once he found his true self all his mental and spiritual suffering would end forever, because *Brahman* was the one true reality, eternal and unchanging.

After a long and careful search for his own *atman*, or self, and after a painstaking and dispassionate look at the nature of reality, Buddha came to the realization that as long as the idea of a soul, or the idea of a God, remained, there was no real abandonment of the illusion of self. Buddha found that the illusion of a self, which was some kind of enduring, individual soul, was just as much a cause of mental and spiritual unrest as the illusion of any other kind of lesser self created by the mischievous tendencies of the thinking process. By the creation of a substantial self, which it first calls self, then soul, and finally God, the conceptual nature of the thinking faculty dominates, like a spoiled child, the family of processes which actually makes up a person. And this, Buddha said, was the cause of spiritual and mental frustration. Buddha called his new interpretation *anatman*, or no-self.

The processes that actually constitute what we call a person, such as the material elements and the mental elements, are not capable of frustrating themselves. It is the false attachment to a self that is the cause of mental suffering or unrest. The self suffers whenever its identification is threatened by changes in conditions. When Buddha completely abandoned all illusions of self, he was able to gain true insight into the nature of existence; he was able to live life fully, and without conflict, in the actual reality of the ever-changing present moment.

When Eka, the second zen patriarch of China, said to Bodhidharma, "My soul is troubled; please pacify my soul," Bodhidharma answered, "If you bring me your soul I will pacify it for you." Eka said, "I have searched for my soul for many years but I am unable to grasp it." Bodhidharma said, "There, it is pacified!" In other words, since you are unable to grasp what you call soul, how is it that you can grasp what you call your suffering soul? If your so-called soul is so very illusive that it has escaped you all these years, then possibly this suffering which you claim your soul experiences is just as illusive. Could it be that neither soul nor suffering exists, except in your imagination? Eka was able to realize the truth of Bodhidharma's teaching because he had spent many years in an unsuccessful search for his own soul, or inmost self. This search is very important. It is impossible to experience fully the illusion of self, and the mischief created by it, unless we actually devote ourselves seriously, for many years, to the search for our self.

Someone might say, "I am perfectly happy with myself, so why should I want to give it up, even if it is an illusion?" The concept of a self limits us. The Chinese zen master Huang-po said, "If you conceive of a Buddha, *you will be obstructed by that Buddha*!!! And when you conceive of sentient beings, you will be obstructed by those beings." Psychologists have demonstrated the tendency of animals and human beings to be selectively aware. We tend to see only what interests us. So the more we are attached to some particular concept of our self, the more it will limit our awareness. Freedom lies in the elimination of all concepts of self. Of course, we can't get along in the everyday world without *some* conception of ourself, but we must realize that any concept is only tentative. It is only a partial point of view. No concept can ever provide an absolute perspective. Concepts such as man, woman, child, mother, father, husband, wife, teacher, student, employer, employee, American, Japanese, Christian, Buddhist (all variations of the concept of self) will obstruct our freedom if taken too seriously or rigidly.

Everything is changing. Moment by moment we must redefine ourselves, and the world, by observing what is going on from the point of view of no-self. From the point of view of no-self, or selflessness, the question is: "What is going on?" From the point of view of self, the question is: "What is going on that affects me?" Can you understand the difference?

XI

Time

Another autumn. Wandering today across the dry riverbed, hitting dead stumps with my walking stick. (The hollow ones make the clearest sound.) I stroll leisurely across sandbars and through thickets of cottonwood, alder, and willow until I come to a huge sycamore tree on the bank of the Big Sur River. Here is a good place to sit for a while and wait for time to unfold itself naturally.

On the opposite shore I can see the reflections of the water on the trunks of the trees. Over there the trees are flowing, and here, in a small pool sheltered from the swift current by reed-wrapped rocks, the river is standing still. Thoughts skim lightly over my mind like water striders. They dimple the surface but don't break it. A yellow sycamore leaf falls into the river. I drift along with it into a time-space that has no duration or distance. . . .

A crow caws, breaking the dam of silence and flooding my senses with fresh sounds and colors. My back and leg muscles ache. I get up slowly in a kind of trance and walk upstream to a small bridge that seems to span a river of Vast Emptiness. I see a figure (is it myself?) standing near the bridge on the opposite shore. The figure bends down, scoops a bamboo dipper of water from the river, drinks half, and pours half back into the river.

I recall a friend asking me this question: "Don't you find that time is passing by faster and faster every day?" Since we are almost the same age she is surprised when I answer, "No." I tell her that time is slowing down for me.

In fact, it has almost stopped. But I can remember when I, too, experienced the swift passage of time. When I lived in my old hometown, I always felt that there wasn't enough time to do everything I wanted to do.

Einstein says time is relative. Dogen says time is existence. It is impossible to separate time and existence. Everything is time. These falling leaves are time. These big and small rocks are time. These slender reeds are time. These tiny water striders are time. This river is time, and this bridge over the river is time. I am time, and you are time. Zen Buddhism is time, and modern physics is time.

Everything creates its own time. So the faster we run trying to catch up with time, the faster time runs away from us. The way to slow down time is to slow down ourselves. And the way to stop time, or to transcend time, is to stop ourselves.

Everyone is aware of the ordinary aspect of our lifetime which is called *samsara*. This is the lifetime that has duration and continuity and appears to flow only from past to present to future. But when we stop ourselves completely, we become aware of that other aspect of our lifetime which is called *nirvana*. This is a lifetime that has no duration or continuity. Here life and time flow freely in all directions; from past to present, from present to past, from present to future, from future to present, from present to present, from future to future, from here and now to once-upon-a-time.

Until we arrive at the complete view of our lifetime, we feel like a thirsty man in the middle of a dry desert. But once we arrive at the full reality of our own timelessness and selflessness, we feel as if we have tasted pure water direct from the source of the river of eternal peace.

I kneel down and scoop a handful of cold, clear water from the Big Sur River. I drink half and allow half to slip through my fingers and return to the river. Walking back the way I came, across the dry sands, I shake my dripping hands on a dead stump. Deep in the roots a dragon murmurs.

How much time should one spend sitting in *zazen*? Suzuki Roshi generally advised his students to sit forty minutes twice a day. But after observing the practice of a group of middle-aged, middle-class zen students in my old hometown, he told them, "I think that if you try to do *zazen* once a week, that will make you busy enough." He pointed out the tendency of modern-day Americans to become busier and busier. He said that his American students often became so interested in zen that instead of simplifying their lives they added more complications. Suzuki Roshi told these students that if they worked too hard at zen practice they would not be successful. He likened the practice of *zazen* to that of making bread and said, "You have to mix it little by little, step by step, and moderate temperature is needed. You know yourself quite well," he told them, "and you know how much temperature you need."

At that time I didn't know myself very well, and so I didn't know how much temperature I needed. I didn't even know what kind of bread I was. It took many years of experimenting with myself to find out just how much *zazen* was the right amount. I spent six years watching myself under the influence of a great many periods of *zazen*. Later I spent a year and a half watching myself under the influence of no *zazen* at all. In trying out many different amounts of *zazen* over the years, I came to know myself much better. I found out how much temperature was right for me.

I also found many other similarities between zen practice and bread making. Like the leavening one uses. I discovered that the occidental brand of yeast called love was much too frantic and intoxicating to leaven zen bread. I found that the oriental brand of yeast called compassion was slower-acting, steadier, and more dependable. And I found out that while some zen masters and students were especially talented in the long slow kneading process (integrating the various ingredients of zen into a strong, smooth, resilient character), other zen masters and students were specialists in the quick punch-down (deflating the ego in one swift blow after the warming period had doubled it in size). I was very fortunate to have had both kinds of zen masters: Suzuki Roshi, master of the slow kneading process; and Tatsugami Roshi, master of the quick punch-down. In time, zen students learn to knead themselves and punch themselves down. But it takes a long time and many half-baked or burned loaves in the oven of real-life experience before we begin to get the knack of baking our own zen bread.

I think there may be three kinds of zen students: store bought, homemade, and sourdough. When a person reads about zen without practicing it, he is buying store-bought zen. When a person starts to practice *zazen* under the guidance of a good zen teacher, he is learning to make homemade zen. But when a person becomes his own zen teacher, he is able to make sourdough zen. The zen master provides the yeast in the practice of the beginning student. But when a zen student has found his own storehouse within himself, one tablespoon of the zen master's yeast can be made into a sourdough starter. When continually replenished from the student's own practice, sourdough starter can leaven thousands of loaves of zen bread for many, many years. The greatest sourdough zen master of all was the sixth zen patriarch, Hui-neng. He took one tablespoon of the *Diamond Sutra* as the basis for his starter. Hui-neng's sourdough starter has been carefully used, replenished, and passed on from master to master. It is still fresh and active today.

I don't want to suggest that sourdough zen is *better* than store-bought or homemade zen. I think it is good to taste all three kinds of zen, and then, even though you find one kind suits you more than another, there's no reason not to change your zen habits once in a while so your zen doesn't get stale.

If we look upon *zazen* as a means to an end, we are apt to think that the more *zazen* we do, the closer we will come to gaining enlightenment. There is a zen saying: "One inch of *zazen* is one inch of Buddha." If we are very ambitious, then it may take many thousands of miles of *zazen* to become a big Buddha. But if we are satisfied to be a small Buddha, then one inch of *zazen* may be enough. Actually, there is no comparison in zen between big and small, a lot or a little. One inch of Buddha is enough, and ten thousand miles of Buddha are also enough. A big Buddha is a big Buddha; a small Buddha is a small

Buddha. A lot of zazen is a lot of zazen; a little zazen is a little zazen.

If we are in a big hurry to become enlightened, it may take many more periods of zazen than if we are not in such a rush. There is a story about a young man in Japan who was in a hurry to become a swordsman. When he asked a famous master of swordsmanship how long it would take to become proficient in the craft, he was told that it would take the rest of his life. The young man did not want to wait that long, so he asked the master how long it would take for a person who was willing to work very hard. He was told that it might take about ten years. When the young man said that he would be willing to undergo any hardship to master the art of swordsmanship in the shortest possible time, the master said, "In that case, you will have to remain with me for seventy years. A man in such a hurry as you are to get results seldom learns quickly." This reminds me of the fable of "The Tortoise and the Hare." But reaching the goal in zen is not arriving ahead of the other fellow. It is finding out whether we are a tortoise or a hare. Running the race, practicing zazen, is finding our own speed. Finding our own speed is arriving at the goal, and arriving at the goal is finding out that there is no goal, only a starting line.

I heard a specialist in physical exercise say once that when he began the study of exercise, he thought that it was the last pushup that did the most good. But after many years of physical practice, he discovered that it was the first pushup that was the most valuable. I think this may be true of zazen also. The first few minutes may be the most valuable. It is a law in physics, as well as psychology, that once a body or mind is set in motion it tends to keep going in the same direction, and at the same rate of speed, unless some force is exerted upon it to change the direction or speed. Since Americans tend to over-emphasize activity, it usually takes a great deal of energy to slow themselves down to a point where they can sit quietly and be aware of their original nature. The effort of beginning zazen, and the continuing effort of returning to the practice of zazen, take a great amount of energy and resolve, especially when one is involved in the many distractions of everyday life. As long as we live, the interruptions and the attractions of everyday life will tend to take our attention away from the practice of *zazen*, but the effort of returning to *zazen* is actually what develops healthy and flexible zen muscles, not the total amount of time we spend in *zazen* practice.

This may be as good a time as any to interrupt the subject of Time to consider the problem of interruptions. Most teachers of meditation advise beginning students to select a quiet spot, free from distractions, as the best environment for meditation. But advanced students are often encouraged to meditate in more lively surroundings. It is said that the adept in meditation is able to find composure even in the thick of battle. Practice in dealing with distractions is one reason zen masters discourage their students from spending long periods living and meditating in solitude. Since I spend long periods living and meditating in the mountains, my hermit *karma* provides me with a big distraction (Jack) to liven up my mountain retreats.

Perhaps four days out of five, Jack will find himself moved by my *karma* to interrupt my daily meditation period. "Oh," he will say (as if surprised to find me sitting in the middle of the floor with my legs crossed), "I see you're sitting on your ass again. Well, you'll have to excuse me, Mrs. Buddha. I have *important* work to do." The important work usually consists of making a cup of coffee, or a sandwich, or hunting around for the keys to the truck which he says *I* put away in the wrong place. When Jack feels particularly in tune with his Mara role, he'll cackle like a hen and ask me how long before I hatch my egg. (Mara is the Buddhist devil. His job is to try to make us give up our crazy, or dangerous, or silly practice of zen.)

Mara Jack has a big stockpile of dirty tricks ranging from the humorous, to the threatening, to the shocking, to the seductive. Over the years I have tried different ways of handling my big distraction. I have found that the only effective method is by full recognition and acceptance of its Buddha-nature. As soon as you completely accept the

Buddha-nature of the devil Mara, the old devil will begin to take off his mask. Yesterday Jack came in after I had been meditating for about fifteen minutes, but he didn't interrupt me immediately. Instead, he sat down for about ten minutes. Then he announced, "That's enough for today. If I allow you a full period you won't appreciate it. If I cut your time short it will create a demand."

If someone were to ask me today, "What is enlightenment?" I'd say, "Enlightenment is just an unexpected interruption that bursts in on our peaceful meditation." If we haven't learned how to handle small interruptions, we are apt to become disturbed by big interruptions.

It has been my observation that many husbands and wives of zen students and zen masters are forced by their karmic relationship to play the devil's advocate. In zen monasteries students are taught to bow after being hit by the *kyosaku*, or awakening stick. In the privacy of the home the awakening stick, or sword that cuts away illusions, is usually thrust (like it or not) into the hands of the husband or wife. We should try to bow gratefully when struck emotionally or physically by our zen master or our marriage partner. After we have received thirty-two black-and-blue marks and can accept them wholeheartedly, we may begin to manifest a trace of our Buddha-nature.

But to get back to Time. We must be careful not to divide the time spent in the formal cross-legged position of *zazen* from the other activities of daily life. If we spend eighty minutes a day in the formal posture of *zazen*, and then neglect the practice of bringing our mind back frequently and regularly to the actual activities of the moment during the rest of the day, we have missed the point. But if we spend only forty minutes a week in the cross-legged position of *zazen*, and make it a habit to be attentive to our everyday zen practice, then our zen practice will pervade our whole zen environment.

There will be different times in our lives when we will need different amounts of formal *zazen*. One indication that we may need more *zazen* is when we feel sorry for ourselves, or are not satisfied with our lives. By the effort of a little extra *zazen* we may be able to appreciate our life, just as it is, or we may be able to see clearly that it is about time for a change, and our *zazen* will be able to help us move forward smoothly in the direction of things-as-they-are-going. The important thing is not to worry too much about how much *zazen* is enough *zazen*. Just do it, and give it your full attention. And give it your full attention when you don't do it.

XII

Jumping in Over
Your Head

About a month ago I ran into a wall. Nothing I wrote had a spark of life or truth to it. I didn't want to stop writing because I was sure that when I began again I would just have to push through the same impasse. So I kept writing pages of dead words every day. At the same time I was trying to work through this problem, Jack was trying to solve some problems of his own. We were both irritable.

Last Monday Jack came home and asked me a question in the middle of a dead paragraph. I didn't stop typing, and I didn't answer him. Even when he's feeling good, Jack doesn't like to hear the sound of the typewriter. It gets on his nerves. He puts little faith in written words and considers reading and writing a waste of real life. So I should have known, but—well, you know how it is sometimes. . . .

Jack picked up my typewriter, took it out on the deck, and threw it as far as he could. It landed a hundred feet down the canyon.

I was furious. It was an excellent typewriter that had been given to me by a friend. Jack and I had a rip-roaring fight that lasted two full days. It's still a little early to tell for sure, but we both feel we made definite progress in pushing through our mental blocks. And he has promised to buy me a new typewriter someday when he makes some extra money. In the meantime I'm using an old typewriter my sister sent me. It has a few mechanical problems, but, considering its age, it writes passable paragraphs. Some even show a spark of life.

Talking or reading about zen is like sticking your big toe in the water. In order to know what zen is all about you have to jump in over your head. One of my zen teachers, Dainin Katagiri Roshi, used to say, "If you want to learn how to swim just jump into the water and the water will hold you up. If you want to learn how to do *zazen* just jump into *zazen* and *zazen* will hold you up." Most of us learned to swim when we were very young, so we may have forgotten the thrill of the first time we jumped into the water over our heads. Even though we held our nose and closed our eyes, we could not help but wonder, as we sank deeper and deeper into the water, if we would ever come up again. But just as we were about to give up hope, we found ourself floating back up to the surface again. Later, after we learned to trust the water, we discovered that when we relaxed, we could float. The water held us up. No matter how many times we may have seen the water support other swimmers, we will never have complete trust in the water until we have experienced directly the water's support for ourself. And it is not until we have actually experienced the fact that *zazen* will hold us up that we really know what this means.

When we are talking or reading about zen, we are standing at the edge of the water, testing it out with our big toe. When we are trying to practice *zazen*, we have jumped into the water over our head. And when zen has been fully integrated in our life, we are floating comfortably on the surface of the water—not all the way in and not all the way out. The world above the water is the realm of ordinary consciousness, the realm of everyday life. The world under the water is the realm of sorcery and magic, the world of mythology, miracles, and madness. To know only the world above the water is to be caught in the realm of ordinary men. To spend too much time under the water is to be caught by the spells of sorcery.

The time when we have jumped into zen over our head

is a very strange, and sometimes frightening, period of our life. The first half-dozen years of practicing *zazen* are apt to be filled with various kinds of emotional, intellectual, physical, and psychological problems. When we jump into *zazen*, headfirst, we often make such a big splash that friends and relatives get their images of us dampened. To those standing on the sidelines it may seem that *zazen* is making us very confused. And we may sometimes think that our friends may be right. As we sink down into the depths of our mind, with our eyes open, we become aware of phenomena that we had not noticed before.

But the phenomena that we encounter in our mind, and the problems that we encounter in our daily life that *zazen* seems to intensify, are like bubbles that we see under the water, or like drops of water that are splashed on the bystanders. If we continue to practice *zazen* we will find that the problems in our mind will float to the surface and dissolve. And if we continue to practice *zazen* we will find that the problems in the minds of our friends and relatives will evaporate without having caused them any permanent damage.

When we first begin the practice of *zazen*, we may feel very awkward. Nevertheless, even if the best we can do is a belly flop we need not feel ashamed of our style. A zen teacher of mine often quoted her Japanese tea master who told his students, "If you're born clumsy it's not bad, and if you're born clever it's not good. The proper way to serve tea is to find your own way." This is the attitude we should cultivate when we practice *zazen*. If we are clumsy at *zazen* it is not bad. If we are clever at *zazen* it is not good. The proper way, the only way to practice *zazen* is to find our own way. We just have to jump into *zazen*, and *zazen* will show us our way.

I encountered many emotional and psychological problems in my zen practice. Sometimes it seemed as if I were getting in so far over my head that I might drown myself in my mental problems. Sometimes my behavior bewildered my companions and zen teachers. But as I continued to practice *zazen*, and to sink deeper and deeper into the confusion of my own mind, I discovered that no matter how low I sank, *zazen* always brought me safely back up to the surface again.

It was not until I left all my zen teachers and all my zen companions, however, that I learned to trust *zazen* completely. When I put all my trust in my own *zazen*, I was able to stop comparing my zen practice with the zen practice of other students or teachers. I was able to give up discriminating between crazy zen practice and sane zen practice, between poor zen practice and good zen practice, or between wrong zen practice and correct zen practice. When I put all my trust in my own *zazen* I was able to give up thinking about how to practice *zazen* and let *zazen* do what it wanted with me. Relaxed, I found myself floating calmly on the surface of my own confusion.

We should not feel surprised or frightened if we encounter disturbing physical or mental phenomena now and then during our zen practice. The condition is not uncommon. In fact, some spiritual disciplines seek to intensify and prolong contact with this level of experience. In Carlos Castaneda's accounts of his training under the Yaqui Indian, don Juan, he tells of the cultivation of this level of consciousness through the use of peyote and other psychotropic plants. But once he becomes familiar with the world of don Juan's sorcery, Carlos Castaneda's teacher warns him that this drug-altered consciousness is not the world of *seeing* (or, as Buddhists would say, seeing-things-as-they-are). The purpose of using the psychotropic plants is only to help the student give up his strong attachment to perceiving the world through his rigidly conditioned mind.

In his book *Journey to Ixtlan*, Carlos Castaneda tells of an experience he had one day when he found he could "talk" to a coyote. Castaneda's teacher explained that this is what happens to a sorcerer's apprentice when the ordinary world "stops." Usually we look at the world through the thinking mind which has been conditioned to see it in the ordinary way. From the day we are born we are told what the world is like; so we see it only through this screen of ordinary thoughts. When Castaneda found that he could talk to a coyote, he had simply acquired the ability to experience the world in the way don Juan had been training him for years to experience it—through the mind of a sorcerer. In the world of sorcerers, animals and all other living things are able to talk.

Don Juan cautions Castaneda to be careful not to get attached to the sorcerer's world. The aim of don Juan's teaching is to help the student learn to *see*. *Seeing*, according to don Juan, is the art of sneaking between the worlds. In Zen Buddhism, seeing-things-as-they-are is experiencing everything with an unconditioned mind.

When we begin the practice of zen, mountains and rivers and coyotes are just ordinary mountains and rivers and coyotes. After we have learned to look at the world through the eyes of Buddhism, mountains and rivers and coyotes are no longer just ordinary mountains and rivers and coyotes. They become extraordinary. But when we fully realize the practice of zen, mountains and rivers and coyotes are just mountains and rivers and coyotes, not ordinary and not extraordinary.

In the practice of *zazen*, visions and strange mental states such as hallucinations, called *makyo* in Japanese, are considered obstructions to meditation. When these mental conditions affect our behavior, we may find ourselves freaking out in some way or other. Hakuin, the founder of the Japanese Rinzai zen school, spoke of his long and difficult encounter with the kind of psychological disturbance familiar to medieval contemplatives. From the knowledge of himself, which he learned from what he called his zen sickness, Hakuin became a strong and effective zen teacher. Dr. Edward Conze, the Buddhist scholar, says that the *tantras* (secret meditations) of Tibetan Buddhism evolved, to some extent, to cope with the psychic disturbances encountered in the development of the spiritual life. Dr. Conze says, "The complacency of people who never exert any pressure upon themselves is startled, and secretly gratified, by the spiritual, mental, and physical disorders of those who really attempt to do something. These disturbances, like the 'Dark Night of the Spirit,' [a prolonged state of spiritual depression] are not signs of failure, as the untutored worldling is apt to suppose, but signs of growth—the creaking of rheumatic joints foretelling their eventual mobility."

The important thing in encountering any kind of unusual mental or physical phenomena is to let it come in and let it go out. If you try to prevent this kind of activity it will control you unconsciously. If you become fascinated by this kind of activity it will control you consciously.

The founder of the Christian Science method of faith healing, Mary Baker Eddy, observed that many of her patients exhibited disturbed physical and mental disorders just prior to their complete recovery. She called this condition "chemicalization" and believed that it was caused by the poisons of error or illusion being expelled from the mind by the light of truth. Perhaps the classic example of psychic disturbance in Buddhism is the period just prior to Gautama Buddha's enlightenment under the Bodhi Tree, when the hosts of Mara (the spirit of evil or ignorance) assaulted Shakyamuni with temptation and terrors.

I think Mrs. Eddy's term "chemicalization" is a good description of what happens to us sometimes when we practice *zazen*. When we extend the truth of *zazen* deeper and deeper into the dark regions of the mind, it is like dropping an Alka-Seltzer tablet into a glass of water. Thousands of tiny bubbles begin to disturb the water. But after the Alka-Seltzer tablet and the water are completely mixed the bubbles disappear, and the water becomes clear again. When the truth of *zazen* sinks down into our mind, it creates bubbles of confusion which temporarily cloud the mind. But after *zazen* and mind are fully blended, the confusion disappears. When we drink the mixture of Alka-Seltzer and water, we settle our upset stomach. When we digest the mixture of *zazen* and life, we settle our upset mind.

XIII

Mud Puddles

When we bow to the floor in Zen Buddhism, we do not bow to some Buddha outside ourselves. It is our ego that bows before our original nature. Suzuki Roshi once told a story about the origin of the Buddhist bow. He said that one day Buddha was walking along the road and came to a muddy spot. A woman with long hair, seeing that Buddha had to cross the muddy place in the road, bowed down so that her long hair covered the puddle, enabling Buddha to pass over the hindrance without getting dirty.

In this story the woman with the long hair represents our ego. And Buddha represents our original nature. As long as we live we will have an ego. When zen monks shave their heads, it is a way of expressing their intention to get rid of their ego. Actually, as Suzuki Roshi explained, a shaved head represents a minimum of ego. Everyone has a trace of ego. Our ego is not necessarily something bad. It is only when we get permanently attached to our ego and think it belongs to us that we will have problems with our ego. If we think our ego belongs to us, then we will become possessed and dominated by our ego. In the act of bowing, our ego comes into direct contact with the muddy spot in the road, with its own imperfections, with its faults. But as soon as it does so, it allows our true nature to pass over those imperfections and faults. When we fully accept the ego and its faults, then Buddha-nature invites the ego to accompany it along the road of enlightenment.

130

The full bow begins in the standing position. The heels are separated slightly, the width of our own fist, and the toes are in line with the centers of our breasts. The hands and arms are in the position of *gassho*. Keeping the hands together until the knees touch the floor, the hands (palms up) and the forehead touch the floor together. The wrist is slightly raised. (Only the fingertips and the elbow area of the forearm actually contact the floor.) The fingertips will almost touch the head, while the elbows will be a few inches from the thighs. Now lift the hands to the level of the ears, and then lower them to the floor again. This lifting and lowering movement is repeated three times. Finally, lift the forehead from the floor, and bring the hands together as the body is raised to the standing position.

In zen temples and monasteries the bows are often performed very quickly, sometimes three and sometimes nine times in a row. But when a zen student is alone, he should slow down the pace of the bow until it is harmonized with his breathing. This allows the student to appreciate fully the act of bowing. Particular attention should be given to lifting the hands off the floor.

I once heard a visiting zen teacher to Tassajara complain about Suzuki Roshi's practice of lifting his hands three times. This zen teacher felt that lifting them once was enough. Suzuki Roshi explained that the act of lifting our hands raises our Buddha-nature. He said we should feel as if Buddha were standing on our hands, and this would help us take care to lift our hands carefully. But Roshi never explained, to my knowledge, the significance of lifting the hands three times. For a long time I tended to agree with the visiting zen master that once was enough. But zen life taught me otherwise. Now I realize that only after going through the three stages of zen training and experiencing fully for ourselves what it means to bow down in humility—not just once but three times at least—and to be lifted up again—not just once but three times at least—from our humiliating position will we be prepared to accept the sixteen-foot-high stature of our own Buddha-nature.

Raising our hands during the bow, lifting our Buddha-nature just slightly off the ground, may also be a way of expressing the true position of zen. The Zen Buddhist aim is not to fly off to some heavenly realm. The aim of zen practice is not to convert human beings into saints or angels, but only to convert half-awake human beings into fully awake human beings.

Of the six psychological realms of Buddhism it is said that only in the human realm are beings able to realize their Buddha-nature. Most of us have been taught by our parents and teachers that angelic beings or saints are closer to God (good) than human beings. In the Christian religion, however, Lucifer, a fallen angel, reminds us of the weak position of the heavenly realms. If we imagine a seesaw with an angel sitting on the high side and a devil sitting on the low side and a human being sitting smack in the middle, at the balancing point, we may have a picture of Gautama Buddha's Middle or Human Way.

One of the most refreshing and enlightening qualities about zen teachers is their complete candor in discussing their faults. They accept their faults with the same attitude as they accept their virtues. No great fuss is made over them.

"Judge not, that ye be not judged." This is good zen psychology. But somehow this sound psychological and spiritual truth has been misinterpreted by many Christians to mean only that we should not judge others. Christians often tend to judge themselves harshly. Saints are sometimes the worst offenders. The saint often punishes himself when he falls below the level of his ideal, which is not to become human, but to become superhuman. It may be easier for a camel, or even an elephant, to go through the eye of a needle than for a saint to realize his true nature. And yet with Buddha-nature, all things are possible—even zen saints.

Suzuki Roshi had a number of small human imperfections. Like an ancient and rare Japanese tea bowl, he had been broken and mended many times. One of Roshi's most troublesome "faults" was his absentmindedness. Sometimes he would become so involved in what he was doing that he would forget his hat or his coat or his briefcase. He often forgot appointments. People laugh at absentminded professors, but an absentminded zen master is not a laughing matter. A master of zen, according to what we read, is supposed to be mindful. Right mindfulness is the seventh step in Gautama Buddha's Noble Eightfold Path of Right Living. Suzuki Roshi said that when he was younger he tried everything he could think of to overcome his embarrassing habit of absentmindedness. But finally after years of failure he gave up and accepted himself just as he was. He stopped taking himself so seriously. When he accepted himself, including his "fault," he transcended the limitations of ordinary mindfulness and entered the realm beyond dualistic categories of absentmindedness and present-mindedness.

When a zen teacher admits his imperfections and faults to his students, he simply accepts things-as-they-are. Here is a muddy spot on the road. It must be crossed before we can continue on our journey. But there is no need to sit down and wallow around in the mud. The teacher simply bows by revealing his fault. This allows the student and teacher to pass over the hindrance uncontaminated. In this way the zen student learns how to accept his own faults.

Everyone will have one or two worst faults. These give us something to work on during our life. My own worst fault may be faultfinding. There is a tendency, I think, to believe that some faults are worse than others, that killing or stealing, for instance, are worse than becoming intoxicated. This may be true in the ordinary world, but in the world of the spirit all faults are equally created. Some of the Buddhist precepts (not to kill, not to steal, not to lie, not to become intoxicated, and not to indulge in unlawful sexual relations) will be easy for us to observe, while others will be much harder or almost impossible. But it is the amount of effort that we devote to working on our particular faults that is important, not the particular kinds of faults we have. If there is one worst fault it may be not having any faults. A person who doesn't have any faults finds it very difficult to sympathize with the faults of others.

If we try to avoid the muddy spots in the road we lose our way. Every spring, puddles cover Buddha's path.

Bowing to our human failings, we realize—it is the fault that makes the Buddha. Zen perfection always includes a trace of imperfection.

Tonight is our last one in this house that we've been caretaking for five months. Tomorrow the owner returns from her travels. It is impossible to live in someone's house without getting to know that person more completely. The warm hospitality of this comfortable home fills every room and spills over like bright blooming plants into the garden around it.

I'll miss the little patio just outside the kitchen door where it is so pleasant to sit in the morning sun, nursing a cup of coffee. I'll miss the deck overlooking the canyon where it is tempting to spend whole afternoons, reading and relaxing in an easy chair. I'll miss the pots of begonias and geraniums. I'll miss the hummingbirds, the woodpeckers, and the family of raccoons that take their regular evening begging practice as seriously as Buddhist monks.

This zen life of ours is so rare and wonderful that it is difficult to leave it. But we must encourage ourselves to begin a new practice. And so tomorrow we will move to the top of the mountain ridge behind Big Sur. We will be caretaking the cabin on Marble Peak that has the oak tree in the front garden. I can't help wondering about the karmic justice that moves us to return to the place where I met the enlightened tick. Is this the karmic penalty for killing a tiny black Buddha?

PART THREE

Cultivating
the
Zen
Environment

I

Where Man Is a Visitor

We're on Highway One between Bixby Creek and Hurricane Point headed south from a town trip to Monterey. Betsy Lou, our twenty-two-going-on-twenty-three-year-old Chevy pickup, is swinging along the curves at a comfortable clip. Betsy Lou is in good shape for her age. She's got all her own glass, stock bumpers and hubcaps, good seat covers, new windshield wipers, and new recaps. Her body's still trim. A couple of months ago Jack and I gave her a coat of paint that looks pretty professional from a distance. Rustoleum brown. You can hardly tell we used a paint brush. Betsy Lou's six cylinders and four gears pull a heck of a load in the backcountry. The one she's packing today is average: a thirty-gallon tank of propane, a heavy box of tools and spare parts, camping gear for the two of us, and a month's supply of groceries.

I can't get over what a fantastically beautiful day it has been. Warm and calm. Like May instead of December. But then, you can never predict the weather from one day to the next on the coast of Big Sur. Or what the ocean will be like. The ocean is always going through her changes. From grumpy gray moods, when she lets it all hang out, to tender turquoise moods like the one today, when she strokes and caresses the rugged coastal mountains, sending good vibes up and down the ridges and deep into the canyons. The affair this ocean and mountain range have going is a romance that'll never grow stale. One day when she's throwing everything she's got at him, and he's stubbornly standing his ground, will be followed by a day when they'll be getting it on again like newlyweds under a thick blanket of fog.

Jack is driving, and we aren't talking to each other. Jack doesn't like to talk when he's driving. When he drives, he likes to concentrate on driving. He's the same when he works. When he works, he likes to concentrate on working. And when he talks, he likes to concentrate on talking. He comes by this zen trait naturally. It's one I've had to cultivate deliberately, by long practice. I'm still not very good at it.

The narrow two-lane highway here is squeezed between an almost vertical cliff above and an almost vertical cliff below. In places there aren't any guard rails, and it's a thousand-foot drop to the beach. From the top of the grade I can catch a glimpse of the gently rolling meadowlands of El Sur. And at the edge of a long curving sandy beach the famous Point Sur lighthouse sitting on top of a monstrous rock.

"Jack, I think I saw a spout off the coast. It might be a gray whale. Do they migrate north in winter or south? I've forgotten."

"I've told you a hundred times that I don't like to talk when I'm driving. If you've got something important to say I'll pull over to the side of the road at the next turnout. Or maybe *you'd* like to drive and let *me* ask *you* questions."

Since I let my driver's license expire years ago, Jack knows this suggestion is guaranteed to shut me up for a while.

"I'm sorry. I won't say another word until we get home."

"If you don't say another word for the next eight months it would be wonderful!"

We come to a bumpy section of road, and my door begins to rattle.

"Is your door closed?"

"I'm not sure."

"That's the trouble with you intellectuals. You spend so

much time reading and writing and thinking that you don't have time to learn how to tie your own shoelaces or close your own doors." Jack has flipped on the right blinker and is pulling off the road. "You know what you remind me of? An abalone. You're tougher than most, Marium, but not too tough for me. When I get through pounding you, I can guarantee you'll be soft enough to cut with a fork."

I open the door a little and close it again. It doesn't catch.

"Slam it, stupid."

I slam it. It catches.

"You didn't have to slam it that hard," Jack snaps, cleverly timing his last remark to come at the moment he creeps up to the edge of the turnout to move back into the line of traffic. "Shut up, now, so I can drive!" he punctuates the conversation.

A woman friend of ours said that she didn't like the way Jack talked to me. Evidently she felt that he didn't treat me with enough respect—the way she felt women *should* be treated. She makes a common mistake. She confuses courtesy with respect. Actually, Jack treats me with the utmost respect. He treats me like an equal. His blunt manner and sarcastic remarks are called grandmotherly kindness in zen. Grandmotherly kindness keeps our illusions of ourself trimmed to a minimum. Many American men treat each other with grandmotherly kindness, but not too many men treat women with equal respect.

We're going downhill again, and Betsy Lou leans into the sharp curves. Jack shifts down to second. The pickup groans and grumbles. Around the next curve there is a sweeping view of the wide mouth of the Little Sur River. The road swings gently down to sea level here, then across a bridge, and completes a half-circle up the other side of the canyon.

A beat-up one-ton truck with high sideboards and an empty bed pulls off the shoulder of the road in front of us. A mongrel dog tied to the cab is barking and clawing at the window, but the cowboy hat (all I can see of the driver through the back window) is ignoring the efforts of the dog to get his attention.

Betsy Lou sputters and coughs as we start up the grade. Jack pulls out the choke and gives her a bit of encouragement.

"Settle down, you old whore. Don't give up on me now." Betsy settles down to a steady whine.

The sandy slopes along the left side of the road are covered with low chaparral and patches of rust-tinged ice plants. In the spring this section of road is a Persian carpet of color.

I said once that Jack was not a man to be judged by ordinary standards. From the beginning I sensed something in him that was out of the ordinary. And as I watched him closely over the years, in his relationship with me and his relationships with other people, I began to appreciate the direct and unpremeditated way he responded to situations.

There are times when Jack responds to situations like a zen master's *nyoi*. *Nyoi* is a Japanese word for the short stubby staff a zen master carries with him. It is the symbol of his teaching authority. Just as every person is a potential Buddha, each zen student is a potential zen master and has an embryonic *nyoi* which will, under perfect conditions, gradually or suddenly be manifested. In the first years of zen training only our zen master will be able to see our embryonic *nyoi*. Later we may begin to feel its effects upon our own behavior; and very much later, perhaps twenty or thirty years later, our *nyoi* may appear in material form where ordinary people will be able to see and feel it clearly.

One day, many years ago, I asked Suzuki Roshi what the Chinese characters on his wooden *nyoi* said. Roshi studied it thoughtfully. After a long pause he spoke, very slowly, as if he were reading the characters one by one: *"Hit him over the head and by his yell you will know if he is a dragon or a snake!"*

Roshi seemed just as surprised by his statement as I, and we both laughed. That was all. We never discussed the matter further. But the words stuck in my mind and slowly, slowly, over many years, those words began to change my mind. The effect of turning words, as they are called in zen, may not be realized immediately or consciously. They may work quietly in the depths of our mind, changing it very subtly. It was only after my zen master passed away that I found out that Suzuki Roshi hadn't read me the inscription on his *nyoi*. He had inscribed the turning words on my own embryonic *nyoi*.

Zen literature is full of examples showing how zen masters use their *nyoi*, or staff, to wake up their students. Here is one of my favorites: One day a student at Tassajara pointed to the *nyoi* of a visiting zen master, Yamada Mumon Roshi, and asked him, "What is this used for?" Mumon Roshi picked up his *nyoi* and scratched his back with it, saying, "It is used for back scratching. It can reach anywhere you want it to." I like this *mondo* (zen question and answer) very much. Zen, like sex, is most fertile when it touches the ridiculous and the sublime in one quick thrust, when it combines the love of being human with the joke of being human.

Even though *nyoi* means literally "as one wishes or thinks," I have a different definition. I say, whatever one wishes or thinks is a *nyoi*. A master of zen can turn anything into a *nyoi* and often does. Here is an example of an unusual *nyoi* used by a Japanese laywoman zen teacher.

"Hakuin used to tell his pupils about an old woman who had a teashop, praising her understanding of zen. The pupils refused to believe what he told them and would go to the teashop to find out for themselves.

"Whenever the woman saw them coming, she could tell at once whether they had come for tea or to look into her grasp of zen. In the former case, she would serve them graciously. In the latter, she would beckon to the pupils to come behind her screen. The instant they obeyed, she would strike them with a fire poker.

"Nine out of ten of them could not escape her beating."

In the right hands a fire poker, or a rolling pin, or a flyswatter can be an effective *nyoi* to hit zen students over the head. By the use of ordinary objects, zen masters and enlightened old women separate the snakes (ordinary beings) from the dragons (awakened beings).

*   *   *

Every dragon has his own teaching style. Suzuki Roshi's style was gentle and kind, like soft spring rain. My second zen master, Tatsugami Roshi, had a powerful and moving style, like an earthquake. Katagiri Roshi had a classic style, impeccable and polished. Kobun Chino Roshi had a charming style, good-natured and innocent. For many years I fought to suppress my natural style. My parents encouraged me to be sweet and kind, and so, at first, I tried to imitate Suzuki Roshi's style. And naturally I failed. Oh, I could fool myself and others for a time, but sooner or later the suppressed energy of my own dramatic style would burst forth to hit some unsuspecting snake or dragon over the head.

Now I accept my own style, even though it doesn't make me terribly popular in my neighborhood. I discovered, by painful experience, that hitting people over the head (hitting them in their ego or their precious image of themselves) can be dangerous. Although some egos fall apart like wet paper bags, others collapse like brick shithouses. So let me warn you—if it is your unfortunate *karma*, like Jack's and mine, to go around like Punch and Judy hitting people over the head, you should be prepared to accept some unpleasant karmic reactions. If you hit a snake, you are likely to get bitten. And if you hit a dragon, you are sure to get burned. But these reactions are what keep your own ego trimmed around the ears. Eventually, as your ego attachments become less rigid, you will find that you have developed an immunity to snakebites and have grown a thick layer of scales to protect you from the scorching fire of suddenly awakened dragons.

(So my woman friend shouldn't worry about how Jack treats me. It may appear that I am getting the short end of the stick—but just wait until we get home! Then's when I'll give him a taste of *my* grandmotherly kindness.)

I once took a seminar led by a Gestalt psychiatrist, the late Dr. Frederick Perls. Now, there was a dragon! Fritz wasn't afraid of being criticized or misunderstood. Fritz had many psychologists and therapists as his students, and he told them: "Don't help your patients. Frustrate them. Push them back to their impasse where they have nowhere to turn. Make them push right through their impasse." This is grandmotherly kindness. A good psychologist, like a good zen master, isn't afraid to drive away the plowman's ox, or to take away the hungry man's food, or to smash bone and take the marrow, or to press the needle and awl into the sore spot. A Chinese zen master said, "When you help someone, you should do your utmost for them; when you kill someone, you should see their blood!"

We're on the long straightaway now just past the Point Sur coast guard station. This is one of my favorite sections of the coast. Here the voluptuously rounded foothills, green in spring and golden brown the rest of the year, draw us closer and closer to home. The road leaves the ocean and cuts through the spacious rolling meadows of El Sur. Fat cattle graze between rows of twisted cypress planted years ago by the first settlers. In the distance is a sweeping view of the Santa Lucia mountain range.

Up there, on top and to the south and east of those dark mountains, is the Ventana Wilderness where Jack and I make our temporary home. "A wilderness, in contrast with those areas where man and his own works dominate the landscape, is hereby recognized as an area where the earth and its community of life are untrammeled by man, where man is a visitor who does not remain." This is a quote I know by heart because I've read it over so many times. It's from The Wilderness Act of 1964.

When you stop to think about it, this whole world, this whole universe, is a kind of wilderness area, a place where man is a visitor who does not remain. And whether we are given a two-week visitor's permit to hike through this wilderness or a ninety-nine-year lease to settle down in it, sooner or later we all have to leave it some day.

After we get to the top of those dark mountains ahead and shake off some of the dust from this town trip, I want to take a closer look at this zen wilderness of transience. I want to find out if it is possible to settle down where there is no settling down, in the place where man is a visitor....

"Marium."
"Yes."

"You're OK."

"Oh."

"You're a good old lady."

"That's nice."

"Don't let it go to your head."

"I won't."

"Now, shut up so I can drive."

II

Fire Clearance

Here in the backcountry the daily chores are simple ones like baking bread, gardening, sewing, or washing clothes. Yesterday I finished digging the last few feet of a new garbage pit that I've been working on for the last two weeks. Jack and I share the digging projects. He digs the shit holes and I dig the garbage pits. Today I'm raking leaves around the cabin. A busy city friend once asked me, "What do you *do* in the mountains?" She filled her time with committee meetings and social events. She said she would be bored to death living day after day in a place where there wasn't anything to *do*. How could I tell her that what I'm doing now (raking leaves) is something to do? My friend feels that it is important for educated people to do something worthwhile. Something that will contribute to the improvement of society. She doesn't consider baking bread, gardening, sewing, or washing clothes important activities. To her, important activities are those that require an education or training. You don't have to be educated to know how to rake leaves. Do you?

A flock of band-tailed pigeons are feeding among the tassels of the oak tree in the front garden. The noise that sounds like a telephone ringing next door is a woodpecker. There aren't any telephones on Marble Peak; no electricity, no mail delivery, or garbage collection. For months after we moved into the cabin there wasn't any water piped to it. But a couple of weeks ago Jack finished the water system, so now we enjoy the luxury of pure, cold mountain water flowing directly from the source of an artesian spring below the cabin to our kitchen sink. And we also now enjoy the luxury of a bathroom with no walls. Our bathtub sits on the side of the mountain and has an unobstructed view of earth, sky, and ocean. On sunny days the water is solar-heated. On overcast days we build a fire under the tub.

A dark shape traveling two hundred miles an hour streaks past my head. All the pigeons scatter. A falcon. Peregrine? It's possible. What a thrill! It reminds me of the time I saw a huge California condor sitting on a rock not far from Half-Dipper Hermitage. Or the time Jack and I spent an hour "barking" and being "barked at" by a rare spotted owl one evening, or the first time I saw a wild boar on the road ahead of me, or the time I watched a pride of mountain lions (through binoculars) crossing Tin Can Ridge. Catching a glimpse of a rare or endangered species is like catching a glimpse of *satori*. It always comes when you least expect it.

The greatest threat to the environment of people living in a national forest is fire. Every spring, toward the end of the rainy season, each home owner or caretaker of property in, or next to, the Los Padres National Forest (which includes Tassajara and Big Sur) is required to clear the area around all buildings for thirty feet or more. This is a double safeguard. It protects the buildings from a forest fire, and it protects the forest from fires that might start inside a building. A good caretaker considers the task of fire clearance a holy obligation.

The greatest threat to the environment of people living in, or close to, the center of existence is what Gautama Buddha called the three fires: the fire of anger, the fire of illusion, and the fire of greed. The original source of these destructive fires is the energy from our karmic nucleus or inmost request. The original energy is neither good nor bad. When handled with care and respect karmic energy can be channeled properly into peaceful and creative work. But usually our inner fire is not carefully contained; it is diverted into nonproductive or destructive channels.

The practice of *zazen* is the good caretaker that keeps

our mind cleared of inflammable debris. *Zazen* is a double safeguard. It protects us from being destroyed by the karmic reactions of others, and it protects others from being destroyed by our own karmic reactions.

Clearing the mind of accumulated undergrowth, dead wood, and trash seems to move along quicker when we involve our bodies in the same kind of activity. As we gather up all the inflammable debris in our outer environment, burying the trash and sorting out the salvageable materials, the atmosphere of our inner environment improves.

I recently read that poet Gary Snyder's zen master, Oda Sesso Roshi, told him, "Zen is two things; meditation, and sweeping the garden; it doesn't matter how big your garden is." That's pure Japanese zen. American zen is clearing the garden with a McLeod (a heavy-duty rake-hoe used for clearing thick underbrush) and a chain saw for the first three years, with a steel rake and a pruning saw for the next three years, and with a bamboo rake and pruning shears after that. Maybe after three or four generations of clearing American gardens, American zen students will be refined enough to respond to a stiff broom. And the size of your garden *does* matter in America. Americans tend to think big. We must be careful not to try to take care of a garden too big to handle. Instead of trying to take care of the whole world, it may be time Americans gave more attention to cleaning up their own backyard.

Zazen and raking the garden are not just aesthetic practices to improve the appearance of our environment. They are survival practices. Until our whole body and mind are completely infused and harmonized with the source of our karmic nucleus, dangerous emotional radiation will leak out, now and then, to contaminate the atmosphere around us. Uncontrolled emotional explosions can destroy personal relationships. An inner fire clearance, created by the emotional detachment acquired in zen training, can prevent the spread of chain-reaction karmic confusion.

Awareness and acceptance of our own failings act as emotional spark arresters. One time Suzuki Roshi told about a woman student who came to him with a problem. She said she had a terrible temper that she could not control. She wondered if *zazen* would help her get rid of her temper. Suzuki Roshi told the woman that *zazen* could not help her get rid of anything. [It can only help us get rid of our attachments to things.] We can't get rid of the energy in our karmic nucleus. The only thing we can do is try to direct the energy into creative channels. Roshi told the woman to accept full responsibility for her temper and not to ask anyone else to share the blame for it. In this way her temper would not hurt anyone. Instead of saying to her child, "Oh, you make me so angry by doing such and such," the woman should say something like: "Oh, I am so angry. I'm sorry. The anger is my fault and not yours." In this way the moment of anger would quickly pass without creating any further karmic contamination. The misbehavior of the child (if there was any) could be handled as another issue. This would help the child learn how to accept full responsibility for his own mistakes.

Some people have the mistaken idea that a fully enlightened person is never angry. This isn't true. An enlightened person, such as a zen master, is seldom angry, but when he *is* angry he uses the anger effectively to cut away the illusions of a particularly stubborn ego attachment. A zen master's anger is not like ordinary anger. Ordinary anger burns good healthy emotional tissue. Enlightened anger cauterizes old emotional wounds.

I remember one occasion when I felt the heaing power of Suzuki Roshi's anger. It was during the period when I was living in my old hometown. I woke up one Sunday morning hungover from a depression which had arisen the day before. I felt lonely, rejected, and sorry for myself. I drove to San Francisco to participate in the services at Sokoji Temple. In the middle of *zazen* Suzuki Roshi began speaking. His voice was very stern. He said: *"If you feel sorry for yourself you should be ashamed!"* Then he strode around the *zendo* and gave every student a smart slap on the shoulder with his *kyosaku* (a long flat stick used to keep students awake during *zazen*). I began to cry. I recalled, for the first time in many years, my mother saying to me as a child, "You should be ashamed of yourself!" By the time my tears stopped, my depression had disappeared. Roshi's scolding apparently cauterized an old emotional wound I had magnified as a child. From that time on I have never been troubled by the destructive fire of self-pity.

Why did Roshi hit all the students in the *zendo*? Perhaps they were all feeling sorry for themselves; or perhaps Roshi did not want to single me out for public chastisement. Suzuki Roshi's students all understood the spirit of being hit by the *kyosaku*, or awakening stick. This zen practice is not punishment. Manjusuri's sword (another name for the *kyosaku*) is the sword that cuts away illusions. The smoldering fire of illusion, like the flash fire of anger, can destroy our appreciation of life. My self-pity was an illusion, a smoky memory that created poor visibility in my inner environment. When we feel sorry for ourselves, we view our present situation through the smoke screen of some childish fantasy. Roshi's enlightened anger was skillful emotional fire fighting. But playing with fire is dangerous, so only a trained emotional fire fighter should attempt to fight fire with fire.

On one occasion I became very angry with Suzuki Roshi. The situation which ignited my anger is not important. It is enough to say that Roshi had made an administrative decision which I felt was completely wrong. I knew that if I allowed the matter to go unchallenged I would lose my respect for myself. This was during the period when I was living in my old hometown. One day I asked Roshi if I could speak to him privately. The two of us sat down, and I told Roshi exactly how I felt about his decision. I am the kind of person who doesn't get angry very often, but when I *do*, the fire of anger burns hot. Roshi listened to my entire outburst without interrupting me. It took about twenty minutes. When all my feeling had been expressed completely, he said very quietly, "Thank you very much." My respect for my teacher (right or wrong) increased immeasurably after this lesson. From that time on I realized the importance of cultivating the most effective emotional fire fighting tool of all—the cooling compassion of mature Zen Buddhism.

If you are a person who is threatened by the fire of

greed, lust, or strong attachments; if you can't seem ever
to satisfy your material or emotional desires, you may find
that your inner and outer fire clearance will have to be
much more extensive than your neighbor's. It is possible
that your inmost request is to follow a religious path. It is
a paradox, but the religious fire often appears first in very
destructive forms. St. Francis of Assisi and Gautama Buddha are examples of spoiled rich kids who found that the
only way they could satisfy their inmost request was to
give up all their material possessions and follow the Man
of No Title along a rather ascetic path. The frustration of
the affluent American society may be a symptom of its
deep desire to return to a simpler, more religious life.

One fellow zen student said that Suzuki Roshi told her
that there is such a thing as bitter zen. The most bitter zen
of all may be the fire of jealousy. Jealousy is not just a
by-product of the materialistic world. In the world of the
spirit, jealousy crucifies the Perfect and tries to assassinate
the Enlightened. *The New Testament* and *The Sutra of Hui-
neng* are recommended reading for anyone who thinks
religion is above political rivalry.

Hui-neng, like Jesus and Buddha, was a revolutionary
religious spirit. At their first meeting, Hung-yen, the fifth
Chinese zen patriarch, recognized the spiritual genius of
the illiterate woodcutter. The Fifth Patriarch observed of
Hui-neng, "This barbarian is too bright," and advised the
young man to keep his mouth shut to avoid rousing the
jealousy of the other monks. So Hui-neng settled down
near the monastery kitchen. He managed to stay out of
monastic politics for a while by keeping busy pounding
rice and splitting firewood.

One day the Fifth Patriarch announced a contest in
which all his disciples could try to express the level of
their enlightenment by submitting a short poem to him.
The head monk was the only one who entered the contest, and even he was so unsure of his spiritual insight
that he secretly wrote his poem on the monastery wall.
He told himself that if the Patriarch approved of his poem
he would claim it as his own.

When someone read the head monk's poem to Hui-
neng, the illiterate woodcutter knew the head monk was

not fully enlightened. Hui-neng composed a poem of his own and asked a visitor to write it on the wall. When the other monks read Hui-neng's poem they thought he had won the contest. But, in order to avoid rousing the jealousy of his older disciples, the Patriarch did not publicly approve of Hui-neng's poem or acknowledge his enlightenment. Instead, the Patriarch secretly passed on his robe of succession to Hui-neng, and advised the woodcutter to leave the monastery as quickly as possible.

Hui-neng hid out in the backcountry, living with a group of hunters for fifteen years. Then, thinking that the bitter fire of jealousy had cooled down enough, he entered the marketplace to begin his teaching career. But even after he had become abbot of his own monastery, Hui-neng's bitter *karma* came back to persecute him. It is said that his enemies set fire to the wood where he was hiding, and he barely escaped by making his way to a rock which later became known as the Rock of Refuge. The Rock of Refuge is said to have the knee prints of the Sixth Patriarch on it. In *The Sutra of Hui-Neng* we learn that the fire of jealousy is controlled by the attitude of humility. Anyone who vows to pursue zen to the bitter end should remember this warning: If you can't stand the heat, stay out of the monastery kitchen.

III

The Three Treasures

Sometimes, when the days are long and hot, and my creative spirit begins to droop like a thirsty plant, I walk down the old road to the source of the Marble Peak spring. At the end of the road I take the little trail that winds down into a cool canyon. At the base of a huge sycamore tree, the spring flows right out of the ground. Here I satisfy my thirst before I walk downstream. Through the trees I can see a waterwheel turning. It's just a rusty iron hay-rake wheel with a dozen iron sand-scoops welded onto its rim. A wooden flume, made from some old boards, channels the creek so that the water hits the scoops and turns the wheel. The turning wheel operates the pump, which pushes the water up the mountain through a pipe to a tank above our garden.

The water flowing over the wheel into the metal scoops creates a soothing, musical sound. It clears my mind of old attachments; it lifts my spirits; it turns me back to the source of creativity. What other Buddha could more eloquently preach the *dharma*?

In Buddhism, a wheel is sometimes used to symbolize the Buddhist teachings. Buddha's first sermon is said to have turned the wheel of the *dharma*. When Buddha realized enlightenment under the Bodhi Tree, he was a *dharma* wheel at rest. When the *dharma* wheel is at rest, it is possible to examine intellectually each separate spoke of the wheel, or each one of its complex meanings. But a *dharma* wheel isn't fully functioning unless it is turning. When Buddha was moved by his inmost request to go to Deer Park near Benares and try to express his enlightenment to the five ascetics who had been his spiritual companions for many years, he set the *dharma* wheel in motion.

It isn't necessary to have a brilliant mind or a spectacular enlightenment to set the *dharma* in motion. If we can just get one spoke of our rusty old wheel moving, then all the other spokes will begin to move. Whenever we do what we know we should do, with our whole body and mind—not just for ourselves but for everyone, and not just for some gaining idea but for the sake of itself—we set the *dharma* wheel in motion.

The wind whispers in the pine trees and rattles the dry leaves of the madrones. A hawk circles overhead; thin clouds drift up from the sea. Walking up the old road I see fresh deer spoor and tracks of a fox in the dust. When we stop seeking for treasures at the end of the road, we find treasures scattered along every inch of the way.

There is a zen story about the son of a thief who asks his father to initiate him into the secrets of the trade. The old thief takes the young man to a big house and while the family is asleep leads the boy quietly to a room which contains a large clothes closet. The father tells his son to go into the closet and pick out some clothing. When the boy is inside, the father closes the closet door and locks it. The father then goes outside and knocks loudly on the front door of the house, waking the residents. Before anyone in the house has a chance to see him, the wily old thief slips quietly away from the scene. The young man in the closet has to summon all his ingenuity to escape from his predicament without getting caught. When he finally manages to reach home safely, the boy begins to berate his father for betraying him; but the old thief interrupts his son, asking him how he managed to get out of the trap. When the son tells his father the details of his escape, the father says, "There you are, you have learned the art."

This is a very interesting story. The author, Wu-tsu Fa-yen, was a zen master who lived in China during the

Sung dynasty. He said, "If people ask me what zen is like, I will say that it is like learning the art of burglary." There is an old riddle from another land that could be added as a commentary to this story. The riddle goes like this: "What is the first thing a thief does when he enters a house? Answer: He looks for a way out." We might say that the adept in zen is someone who has learned how to escape all the traps of life, including the trap of zen.

Kitano Gempo was a Japanese zen master who understood very well the art of not getting caught in three of life's most dangerous traps: pleasure, power, and success. Kitano Gempo said that when he was a young monk he was introduced to the relaxation of smoking. But after enjoying a few pipes of tobacco he realized that smoking might disturb his meditation, so before it became a habit he threw away the pipe and tobacco and never again indulged in this kind of pleasure. A few years later Kitano Gempo became interested in the *I-Ching*, the Chinese doctrine of the universe. Kitano Gempo found that with the aid of the *I-Ching* he was able to tell the future. But after a few successes he decided that he might become so involved in the fascinating aspect of fortune-telling that he would neglect his meditation. So he gave up the study of the *I-Ching* and never again resorted to this kind of power. When Kitano Gempo was twenty-eight years old, he studied calligraphy and Chinese poetry. He became very skilled in these arts, but he realized that if he did not stop he would become a poet and not a zen master. So he never wrote another poem. Kitano Gempo became abbot of Eiheiji Temple in Japan and died at the age of ninety-two after a long life of teaching zen.

Tosui, another famous Japanese zen master, understood the art of not getting caught in the trap of zen. It is said that one day, at the height of his popularity, Tosui disappeared. No one could find him—until years later when one of his disciples discovered him living with some beggars under a bridge in Kyoto. When the disciple asked Tosui to take him again as a student, Tosui said that he would consider doing so—if the student could accept the zen master's life-style. The zen master probably guessed that the student considered himself quite advanced in his understanding of zen, and this was the master's way of testing him out. It took less than three days of Tosui's *tangaryo* for the student to show his disgust with the living conditions and practices at Tosui's tiny temple. (*Tangaryo* is a period of three to seven days spent by novice monks sitting in the monastery vestibule waiting to be admitted.) Tosui found out that the young man was still caught in the trap of discrimination, so the zen master told him, "Get out of here and do not bother me again!"

Now, just because I have mentioned two zen masters who appear to be on opposite sides of the fence, I don't want to leave the impression that Kitano Gempo got caught in the zen trap while Tosui escaped. One zen master escaped the trap of zen by totally rejecting honor and success, while the other escaped the trap of zen by wholeheartedly accepting success and honor. Everyone must escape the zen trap in his own way. It is not until a zen student is able to get himself out of his own traps, by his own ingenuity, that he will find out who he really is and what he is doing in this life.

A zen trap that is apt to catch many zen students is the Buddha's Three Treasures: The Buddha, the *dharma*, and *sangha*. When a zen master says, "Kill the Buddha!" he is warning students not to get caught in the Buddha trap. When Tosui was getting old, a beggar gave him a picture of Buddha. Tosui hung it up in his hut, but he put a reminder to himself underneath. It read: "Mr. Amida Buddha: This little room is quite narrow. I can let you remain as a transient. But don't think I am asking you to help me to be reborn in your paradise." Tosui knew the danger of making Buddha into a kind of god which one seeks to please in order to win a favored position in this life or in the next. It is easy to get trapped by the idea that Buddha is something separate from ourself; and it is just as easy to get trapped by the idea that Buddha is something that is part of ourself. To a beginning zen student Buddha appears as a treasure, but as soon as this happens Buddha turns into an old thief who locks the student in a clothes closet full of fancy robes. After a zen student has been trapped by Buddha for a number of years, he is apt to find the paradise of murderers and thieves much safer than the underworld of Buddhas. But when the zen student realizes thoroughly, by direct experience, that Buddha is a trap, then Buddha turns into a treasure.

Dharma is generally understood to be the teaching of Buddha, or what is popularly called Buddhism. Suzuki Roshi warned his students that if they became the victims of Buddhism *he* might be very happy, but *they* would not. A zen master is constantly trying to point out to his students that the written teaching of Buddhism and zen is not the true teaching. A zen master will say things such as: "Whatever you say, it is not true," or "It is true but not always." He wants the student to understand that truth and reality cannot be limited by words and concepts. After a few years of zen training, the student becomes fairly skillful in avoiding word and concept traps. At this time, however, zen students are apt to fall into another trap. They are liable to mistake some of the practices of Zen Buddhism as permanently and universally valid.

All Soto zen masters put great emphasis upon the practice of *zazen*. I remember listening to a lecture by a visiting Soto zen teacher from Japan who pointed out that the biggest danger in the practice of zen was the danger of giving up *zazen*. I think he was right, but his answer was only partly true. Another danger is that after *zazen* has been practiced for a number of years it may become habitual and formalized. A good healthy vacation from *zazen* can do wonders for the reawakening of a deeper experiential knowledge of the practice. And if the zen student is never moved to come back from his vacation, that's all right too. He may be able to realize himself more comfortably in a warmer or cooler climate. While one person may be liberated by *zazen*, another may find that *yoga*, sensory awareness, gestalt therapy, transcendental meditation, or some other teaching does the trick for him. Zen Buddhism will never be everyone's cup of tea.

In its most limited sense *sangha* means the Buddhist priesthood, or brotherhood; but generally *sangha* is extended to include lay Buddhists, as well as monks and priests. In the ordinary sense a *sangha* consists of a group of three or more Buddhists. It is easy to fall into the conceptual trap of believing that a Buddhist who practices alone, or with just one other person, and who is not officially connected with some kind of Buddhist organization, is not part of the Buddhist *sangha*. But, strictly speaking, from the point of view of zen, our "person" is not limited by our body. It includes all sentient beings. So it *is* possible for one person who is aware of his true Buddha-nature to practice alone in the mountains or in a city apartment and be just as actively participating in the Buddhist *sangha* as someone who lives in a Buddhist commune.

Dependency is one of the *sangha* traps. When we belong to a Zen Buddhist group, it is easy to lean upon our spiritual family for encouragement and support. A group can become a safe haven protecting the timid from encountering the larger environment of zen. Suzuki Roshi often spoke about the necessity of purifying zen. One difference between pure Zen Buddhism and impure Zen Buddhism is that the latter has become an exclusive cult. The members of a cult tend to separate themselves from other religions or beliefs. In time, isolation leads to inbreeding and weakening of the teaching. Each time Zen Buddhism enters a new country, or a new culture, or a new individual, it should strengthen itself by mingling freely in the spiritual marketplace of its new environment.

If we think Buddhists are different from non-Buddhists, we make Buddhism into just another old hometown. According to Gautama Buddha, all human beings are manifestations of original nature. Some are awakened to their original nature, and others are not. Those who are awakened are tentatively called Buddhists or Buddha, and those who are not yet awakened are tentatively called ordinary people or non-Buddhists. But, strictly speaking, every human being is a Buddha or a potential Buddha. And not only human beings, but everything is Buddha-nature. The Buddhist *sangha* is not exclusively limited to the human race. It includes plants and animals and minerals—in short, everything conceivable and everything beyond human conception.

There is a story about a Chinese Buddhist philosopher, Tao-sheng, whose enlightenment was so profound that his contemporaries could not understand it. He was expelled from the Buddhist *sangha* for being a heretic. When Tao-shen found human beings too hardheaded to hear the truth, he lectured to the rocks in the desert. Later Buddhists say that when Tao-sheng told the rocks that they, too, had Buddha-nature, the rocks nodded in agreement.

Today we need more zen teachers who know how to talk to rocks. And we need more zen students willing to listen to rocks. Zen students should be encouraged to explore the outer limits of the Buddhist *sangha* before settling down in their old hometown of human nature. Unfortunately, today, as well as in the past, students or teachers who have a talent for talking to rocks will most likely be considered crazy or heretical. But someday, someone will appreciate this kind of heresy.

IV

Wine Tasting:
The First Cup

When we moved to Marble Peak, Jack didn't know how he would be able to make enough money to fill the gas tank of our old truck or stock the shelves of the cabin. But a few months after we settled in, he heard that some new buildings were to be constructed at the satellite tracking station on Anderson Peak, just a mile away. All summer Jack has been working at the tracking station, and we have saved enough for a winter grubstake. He also got some unexpected fringe benefits: all the form lumber he could haul away. Today Jack is stacking two-by-fours and plywood on stringers so they won't warp. The lumber that is too damaged to use for building sheds or shelves or whatever he'll cut up for kindling.

An old-timer, who had a gold-mining claim in the Los Burros Mining District in Big Sur for many years, once gave Jack a small nugget of zen wisdom: "Pick up little things you find lying around, like a nail or a screw, or a piece of baling wire or an old axhead without a handle. Make a place to keep everything sorted neatly. If you start taking care of the little things now, later the big things will take care of themselves."

Last week Jack brought home an old braided rug that had been abandoned. For two years it had been lying alongside the road in the sun and rain and snow. The young people who hauled it up the mountain left Big Sur before they got around to packing it into the cabin they were caretaking. Now nobody wants it. Except us. The colors of the rug are my favorites—autumn tones of gold, brown, and rust.

This morning Jack helped me spread the rug out on a big piece of plastic sheeting in front of the cabin. While he has been stacking lumber, I have been sweeping the rug and cutting it into usable sections. Some parts are too rotten to save. But others only need to be resewn. It's unpleasant work. The dust dries my hands and cracks my fingers. The deer flies are thick today, and I'm tempted to chuck the whole project. But I encourage myself to stick with it. When I'm finished, I'll have enough rugs to cover the bare floor of the Marble Peak cabin.

"A monk named Seizei asked of Sozan: 'Seizei is alone and poor. Will you give him support?'

"Sozan asked: 'Seizei?'

"Seizei responded: 'Yes, sir.'

"Sozan said: 'You have zen, the best wine in China, and already have finished three cups, and still you are saying they did not even wet your lips.'"

Until we have tasted the wine of solitude, poverty, and insecurity, we have not tasted vintage zen. But even if we have drunk several bottles of the finest zen wine, we may not have appreciated the taste. Seizei could not taste the zen in his cup because it was not Seizei who drank the wine. It was Seizei's conditioned mind, his dualistic thinking mind, that drank the wine. To Seizei's ordinary way of thinking, poverty, solitude, and insecurity tasted like bitter medicine. But, as Hui-neng observed, "That which is of bitter taste is bound to be good medicine."

Ordinary people are strongly attached to the idea that poverty, solitude, and insecurity are evils to be avoided or overcome. Until I was in my early forties I clung to an American dream, the illusion that happiness is the by-product of prosperity, companionship, and security. By the time I reached middle age I had become a member-in-good-standing of the Affluent Society. I had a wine cellar full of the most expensive and most widely advertised brands of California-grown happiness. But I discovered that the extravagant claims of the American wine merchants were misleading. I was no happier *with* prosperity than I had been without it. In fact, it seemed that the happiest times of my life had been the times when I had been the least prosperous.

I began to do some research on the source of happiness, and I found that almost all sages, in all cultures, in all times, agreed that happiness is seldom increased by accumulating possessions but more often by getting rid of them. In order to test this principle I decided to cultivate a life of poverty. The idea of deliberately cultivating a life of poverty may sound crazy to the ordinary American: but in Japan, which, until recently, was a poor country, the cult of *wabi* (a way of life that is poor in spirit as well as poor in material or worldly possessions) is considered to be extremely good taste.

Now, after many years of testing a *wabi* life, I am in a better position to compare my old life of prosperity with my new life of poverty. I can see that the energy required to accumulate possessions, and the energy required to hold on to those possessions, takes away from the energy that can be used to appreciate the actual value of life. During the period in which I was busy accumulating and trying to hold onto my possessions, I didn't have the time, or energy, to enjoy the most precious gifts of all, the ordinary miracles of life. These ordinary miracles are the ones we usually take for granted: earth, sky, water, fire, air, sun, moon, stars, rain, wind, trees, plants, animals—and the miracles of everyday living: eating, sleeping, walking, breathing—in short, the greater part of our original nature.

There is a story about Ryokan, a very poor Japanese zen master, who lived alone in a little hut enjoying nothing but the best zen wine in Japan. When a thief came to Ryokan's hut and couldn't find anything to steal, Ryokan offered him his clothes as a gift. After the thief left, Ryokan sat naked watching the moon. "Poor fellow," he mused, "I wish I could give him this beautiful moon." When we are prosperous, we may be as poverty-stricken as a thief. We have less time to enjoy the moon of our original nature. But after we give away our prosperity we have plenty of time to appreciate our zen environment.

Those who are not poor by choice will probably disagree with me and complain that they are not happy. Most poor people believe that if they could only become prosperous they would find happiness. The reason ordinary people can't find happiness in poverty is that they have been taught to fight poverty. But if we don't fight poverty, or ignore it, or run away from it—if we observe poverty with a mind free of preconceived ideas and false conditioning, poverty will reveal its true nature. The American writer-naturalist Thoreau extolled the value of a life of simplicity in his book *Walden*. St. Francis of Assisi found a friend in poverty. He called his friend My Lady Poverty and wooed his Lady with courtly manners and troubadour songs. This kind of attitude is one in which we are able to appreciate fully the blessings of poverty.

To appreciate poverty in the city may be more difficult than to appreciate it in the country. I can't speak from personal experience about a life of poverty in a city environment. But recently I read a very inspiring account of the life and teachings of Tenko-San (Tenko Nishida), the Japanese founder of the Ittoen way of life which features homelessness, poverty, and selfless service. Members of Ittoen consider the base of their practice the city streets. They go to various households, work out of gratitude, and humbly accept what is offered to them out of gratitude—necessities such as meals, baths, clothes, and lodging. Tenko-San discovered, by personal experience, that God, or Buddha-nature, provides us with everything we need in this life.

The religious genius, Dogen Zenji, observed that each person is born into life with a fixed allotment of life and food. Another religious genius, from another time and place, said the same thing in different words: "Take no thought for your life, what ye shall eat: neither for the body, what ye shall put on.... Consider the ravens: for they neither sow nor reap: which neither have storehouse nor barn, and God feedeth them.... Consider the lilies how they grow: they toil not; they spin not; and yet I say unto you that Solomon is all his glory was not arrayed like one of these."

In my prosperous life I had many modern conveniences, including those most American women now consider necessities: an electric stove, refrigerator, washer and dryer, central heating, hot and cold running water, two inside bathrooms, two telephones, and a television set. In my life of poverty I have none of these conveniences. And I don't miss them. I realize, by experience, that they are mixed blessings. It is difficult to appreciate the actual value of life when it is *too* convenient or *too* comfortable.

There is a zen saying by a Chinese zen layman, P'ang Chushi: "Drawing water; carrying firewood; how wonderful, how mysterious!" There is something uniquely satisfying to the body and spirit in being directly and fully involved in everyday activities. Cutting wood; stacking it; getting out of bed on an icy morning; building the fire; grinding coffee; boiling it over the open fire; drinking it in the presence of the mountain, the sky, and the ocean—all these activities bring us closer to our original nature. A woman appreciates the effort her man has taken to cut and stack a good supply of wood. And he appreciates the effort his woman takes to keep the fire going. They both appreciate the windfalls the mountain provides them; and the mountain appreciates being appreciated. An evening listening to the rain on the roof, and watching the fire, is much more enlightening than an evening watching television. The companionship of fire brings us closer to our original nature.

Until Jack installed the water system on the Marble Peak property, I hauled all the water from a little spring below the cabin, usually making two or three trips a day to supply our basic needs. Carrying water is the ordinary way of life in the backcountry. Having water piped into the cabin is very convenient, but I wonder if it might be *too* convenient. In order not to lose my appreciation for water, I wash clothes outside, below the cabin, using an old-fashioned tub and scrub board. I wring the clothes out by hand; then I carry them up the hill and hang them out to dry on lines stretched between two trees. Ever since I gave up my washing machine and dryer I have learned how much these modern conveniences take away from a woman's natural expression. Washing clothes by hand tends to awaken their original nature. Jack says that whenever he puts on clothes I have washed by hand, they remind him of how much he appreciates me. And every time I throw a log on the fire it reminds me of how much I appreciate him. Our wine jug is empty tonight and it's a long way to town, but that's OK. I've discovered that the best time to taste the zen in our cup is when it's empty.

There may be many who will object to the life I am exploring because they believe it's impossible to go back to the good old days. Manufacturers very cleverly manipulate statistics to sell us on the necessity of continuing in the direction of more dependency upon their products. But if we stop and really look at what-is-going-on we find that it is not only possible to go back, but sometimes it is the only sane thing to do. If we find that the road we have been taking has led us to the brink of disaster, it is only sensible to retrace our steps in order to seek out a better road.

Of course, it is not necessary for everyone to go back to the culture of kerosene lamps, wood stoves, and old-fashioned scrub boards. But unless lots of us step back a little, perhaps just to the point of getting rid of our television (the great mass conditioner and stimulator of the fires of greed, anger, illusion, and fear), and begin using the precious time we all waste watching it in activities that detach us from the net of mass-produced illusions, we may wake up some morning under a mushroom cloud to discover that we have been transported back to the time of the cave dwellers. Ours won't be the first civilization in history that committed suicide because its people lost touch with their original nature.

V

Wine Tasting:
The Second and
Third Cups

It's been another one of those hot muggy Indian summer days when the deer flies—or no-see-ums, as the locals call them—have turned the mountains into a wilderness of irritation. For a week they have been so thick that even bug repellent doesn't help. Mara's army of little devils tickle and torment the sensitive inner linings of eyes, ears, nose, and throat—as well as every inch of exposed skin. The only escape from the torture is inside the cabin. It's like sitting through a seven-day *sesshin*. When your whole body and mind is concentrated on just surviving, there isn't an ounce of energy left over to indulge in daydreaming.

It's evening now, about an hour after sunset. We are sitting on the screen porch, imprisoned within our solitude. The moon is slow to rise tonight. Beyond the balustrade the shadows deepen. The ocean and mountain fade into dark blue emptiness.

Tired of staying here, but if we start wandering again who will keep you company?

There is no answer from the oak tree in the front garden. In the distance, deep from within a canyon, an owl hoots softly. The barometric pressure is beginning to fall. The local weather bird forecasts a cooling trend. As the first watch of the night begins, the mountains heave a great sigh of relief.

Suzuki Roshi often said that to be able to practice *zazen* with a group was the most important thing for zen students. We *are* fortunate when we are able to enjoy the companionship of a group of kindred spirits. But this does not mean that those who practice alone should feel less fortunate. Sometimes circumstances do not permit us to practice *zazen* under a teacher's direct guidance or with the reinforcement of a group. At other times we may be moved by our *karma* to leave our zen teacher and friends in order to practice alone. When we are separated from friends who speak our own spiritual language, we are apt to become very lonely. But if we cultivate this loneliness it can become the fertile ground for true self-supporting Buddhism. The fear of loneliness is an acquired taste. When we cultivate our taste for solitude, we rediscover our original home.

The environment of Big Sur favors the cultivation of solitude. When I was moved to Big Sur by my *karma*, I realized, after a few days alone in Half-Dipper Hermitage, that it had been the first time in my entire life that I had spent even one whole day and night alone—without seeing, hearing, or talking to another human being. And I don't think my case is exceptional. To most contemporary Americans, being alone means being lonely. We fill our solitude with all kinds of distractions: talking to friends on the telephone, listening to the radio, watching television, reading books, or pursuing hobbies. We don't appreciate the real value of solitude—a time in which we can become better acquainted with our original nature. Loneliness is not caused by separation from others; it is caused by separation from our true nature.

The zen ideal, the *bodhisattva*, is one who renounces the bliss of *nirvana* to return to the ordinary world of society to help awaken all sentient beings. The *bodhisattva* spirit has its roots in the life of Gautama Buddha, who rejected a life of solitary contemplation for a life of teaching others. Because of our puritan heritage, many Americans have a tendency to emphasize the value of social activity. Many

American zen students are strongly attached to the *bodhisattva* ideal. From the point of view of someone attached to the *bodhisattva* ideal, the zen hermit may appear to be deficient in compassion, selfishly attached to the bliss of *nirvana*, and unwilling or unable to put up with the distractions and annoyances of ordinary social life. But after taking a swig or two of the solitary life, I found out that the bliss of *nirvana* is no more addicting than the seductions of *samsara*.

During the four months that I lived in Half-Dipper Hermitage and swallowed the dregs of my loneliness, I discovered that living alone was just as disillusioning as living with others. This was the time that I discovered my own uselessness, my own emptiness, my own nothingness. But out of this barren, burned-out ground of being, something that had been lying dormant for many years began to reappear. To know ourselves completely it is necessary to explore both sides of our original nature, the solitary side as well as the social. Until we arrive at the dead end of many relationships on the one hand, and the dead end of no relationship on the other hand, we will not be able fully to experience our true nature, one which transcends both sides—not social and not solitary, not many and not one.

In the Christian religion the social spirit and the solitary spirit are symbolized by the two sisters: Martha, the *bodhisattva;* and Mary, the hermit. Martha, who tries to help all sentient beings, tends to be "cumbered about with much serving" and grumbles that her sister is not carrying her share of the load. Jesus answers the overworked *bodhisattva* by telling her, "Martha, Martha, thou art careful and troubled about many things; but one thing is needful; and Mary hath chosen that good part which shall not be taken away from her." When we fully appreciate both our social *and* our solitary nature, it is like introducing two strangers to each other who then discover that they belong to the same family. When Martha and Mary realize they are only two aspects of one nature, they are able to live together harmoniously.

In the Catholic religion there are retreats for those who feel called to the solitary life. When I was living at Tassajara, I tried to encourage the zen community to provide a place

for zen hermits within the framework of the organization
I was told, however, that it was not in the tradition of Z
Buddhism to support zen hermits. Recently I found o
that in Vietnam zen hermits *are* included in the monast
community. Thich Nhat Hanh, a Vietnamese zen mon
describes the hermit practice in his book, *Zen Keys*. F
says, "A zen practitioner can remain in his coq [hut] thre
years, or one year, or three months, according to h
liking. A novice is appointed to assist him during th
period of intensive zen practice." Nevertheless, in the la
year or two I have begun to appreciate the position of m
own zen teachers. Now I think that any zen student wh
is moved to become a zen hermit should be prompt
thrown out of the zen community.

According to an old Chinese legend, it is said that
mother lion throws her cubs over the precipice soon aft
they are born to see if they are strong enough to clim
back up. Only those who make it back are worthy of
lion's heritage. At first, the cub will expect someone in h
family to come to his rescue. When we jump or ar
pushed by our *karma* into the insecurity of poverty an
solitude, it is quite normal to beg for help. After I wa
expelled from the monastery by my second zen master (
golden-haired lion), I wrote to two zen organizations
had supported in my prosperous years. In abbreviate
form my letters read something like this:

"Dear Zen Community: Marian is alone and poor. Wi
you give her support?"

But my old zen family wasn't able to help me financia
ly. It was very difficult for them to turn down my request
But they realized intuitively that helping a baby lio
wouldn't help him. Zen hermits will never be able t
appreciate their true nature until they get a taste of th
zen wine of nonsupport.

The zen life encourages us to put all our eggs in on
basket, and after we have done so it takes away th
basket. Deserted by our religious family, cut off from ou
old hometown, we begin really to taste our poverty, ou
loneliness, and our helplessness. When we are completel
down and out, at our wit's end, with no place to go—thei
we are ready, for the first time, to settle down where ther

is no settling down. Now we don't care whether we are helped by Buddha or we are helped by the devil Mara. We lose all our false pride; we lose all our false discrimination. When we are grateful for the most humble shelter, the poorest food, shabbiest clothes, and the most miserable company—when we find ourselves *under* the bridge instead of on top of it—we knock once more on Tosui's door. This time the beggar zen master recognizes and welcomes home his old disciple.

VI

Beggar's Mind

The first good rainstorm of the season has given me a chance to get caught up on my letter writing. I've just finished answering one from my oldest daughter who is going through a period of financial difficulties. She probably expects me to sympathize with her "problem." I probably should have told her, "Don't worry about it," as Katagiri Roshi used to say to me when I complained to him about my problems. But my daughter is not me and I am not Katagiri Roshi, so I must answer her in my own way. Since I had no money to put into her empty begging bowl, I was forced to dig deeper into the patched lining of my beggar's mind to see if I couldn't find some turning words that would help my daughter see through her "problem," and help her realize that she has been given a rare opportunity to get a taste of the best zen wine in the country.

By late afternoon there is a break in the storm. I put on my khaki surplus-store raincoat and my tire-patched rubber boots and take a walk up the road toward the meadow where Jack said he would be cutting a dead madrone. Jack loves to work in the rain. When most people would be sitting inside waiting for the rain to stop, Jack gets two or three days' work done. Then when the sun comes out and most people would be working, he relaxes.

Everything smells so clean and fresh! The sky is still overcast, but a break in the clouds allows a thin shaft of sunlight to spotlight a small circle of trees on a distant mountain. The light moves slowly over the ridges and valleys like some celestial being searching for something lost.

I detour by the garden to see how the vegetables are doing. All of them—squash, tomatoes, chard, onions, carrots, cucumbers, parsley, lettuce, broccoli, and cabbage—are trying to climb out of their beds. I dig a hole in the ground outside the garden area. It's damp two inches down. On my way back to the cabin I'll pick some fresh vegetables for dinner. Tomorrow morning I'll pull weeds and cultivate the ground.

By the time I get to the upper meadow, I find that Jack has almost finished splitting a pickup load of firewood. I call to him.

He calls back: "Just in time to help me load the truck!"

In less than a half hour we have the pickup bed filled with a three-week supply of salmon-pink madrone. Here on Marble Peak we are very fortunate to be able to choose between four different kinds of firewood: pine for kindling, madrone for quick hot fires, oak for slow hot fires, and manzanita roots for all-night suckers.

Driving back to the cabin, I tell Jack that the rain has soaked two inches into the ground and ask him if he thinks it's safe to have a fire.

"I was *planning* to build a fire tonight," he answers. Stopping by the garden, I take special care to pick the finest vegetables for dinner. It will be a special occasion. After a long summer fast, Agni, the ancient Indian god of fire, will return to our home to feast on fresh-cut madrone.

A *koan* is a tool which is used to awaken us to our original nature. The practice of *zazen* teaches us the way to handle our *koan*. When we allow a *koan* such as: "Why did Bodhidharma come to China?" to sink into the depths of our mind, it leads us through the mindful activities of our daily life into our inmost request, our karmic nucleus. The seventeen hundred different *koans* are just seventeen hundred different kinds of tools suitable for awakening different kinds of personalities, or different levels of awareness. Each *koan* leads us closer to the original *koan*, the one at the center of our zen environment.

We are the original *koan*. We are the original question.

To know our self is to beg the question. Begging is the way leading to our inmost request and a way of cultivating it. This inmost request is not just a whim of our ego. I is an innate expression of our original nature. It is only because of the activity of the discriminating, dualistic thinking mind that we are not fully aware of our origina *koan*. Strictly speaking, our inmost request is not ours, though we may be something that belongs to it.

Until we awaken our beggar's mind, we will have difficulty awakening our true nature. This is why our zer life pushes us gradually or suddenly over the precipice o our counterfeit life into the nonsupporting realm of reality which early Buddhists called *anitya* (impermanence or transience) and later Buddhists called *sunyata* (emptiness or void). It is the tendency of our human nature to cling to some false idea of permanency. But as long as we hold onto the hope of finding something secure or something permanent, in or outside ourselves, we will not be able to arouse our beggar's mind.

In *The Varieties of Religious Experience*, William James tells about a seventeenth-century Christian woman who embarked upon a life of religious poverty with only one penny in her pocket. But as long as she clung to one penny's worth of faith in her old counterfeit life, God did not help her. It was only after she threw away her penny, and put all her faith in God, that she began to get a taste of God's support. As long as we cling to the idea of something permanent in this life, or the next, we keep a few pennies hidden in the sleeve of our beggar's robe. It is only after we throw away all our counterfeit coins—only after we give up all absolutes, including the concepts of God, Buddha, and self—that we are ready to settle down where there is no settling down, in the time and place where everything is changing.

It is not easy for most Americans to appreciate the religious spirit of the beggar's mind. The Japanese beggar sage, Tenko-San, said that to be truly independent we must be willing to ask for our bare necessities. Usually we think true independence means *not* having to ask for anything, much less having to ask for our bare necessities. But until we are forced to beg for our bare necessities, we are still clinging to some counterfeit idea of ourselves and the world. Bare necessities are not just food, clothing, and shelter. Bare necessities include what is needed to find and cultivate our inmost request. Jesus was pointing to the beggar's mind when he said: "Ask and it shall be given to you, seek and ye shall find, knock and it shall be opened unto you. For everyone that asketh receiveth, and he that seeketh findeth, and to him that knocketh, it shall be opened." At first, we don't know what to ask for, how to ask for it, or whom to ask. *Zazen* is a way to find out what bare necessities are needed to realize our inmost request; *zazen* is a way to ask for the bare necessities; and *zazen* is the one from whom we ask.

As we practice *zazen* we find it easier and easier, as the years go by, to eliminate things and ideas we once thought were essential to our survival. Actually, most of the things we think are essential to our survival are only essential to the survival of our counterfeit self—our ego. But after stripping away our image of ourself, after clearing away unessential ideas and things, we may discover something essential is missing.

Suppose, as in my own case, we find that solitude and poverty are necessary to find, or cultivate, our inmost request. And suppose they are missing from our life. When we feel—in our guts—that it is impossible to realize ourselves without the bare necessities of solitude and poverty, we awaken in our original nature the dormant power of our beggar's mind. When our conscious request and our inmost request are fully harmonized, our intuition and our power are expanded.

Necessity is the mother of intuitive power. Dogen Zenji pointed out, in his essay "Genjokoan": "Understand clearly that when a great need appears a great use appears also; when there is small need there is small use; it is obvious, then, that full use is made of all things at all times according to the necessity thereof." The requests of our ego are small needs, but the requests of our inmost request, our karmic nucleus, are great needs, needs that include everything and everyone. Once we awaken our great need, zen life rushes in to make full use of us. Zen life fills us and fulfills our inmost request.

To the ordinary, unawakened mind, the activities of the inmost request may appear egotistical or selfish. When we are not aware of the true nature of our karmic nucleus, it is difficult to understand what pushes us to do certain things. Our thinking mind jumps to the conclusion that whatever we do is done for some ordinary, logical reason. If it is difficult for our unawakened mind to understand our *own* inmost request, it is often impossible for us to appreciate the true nature of the inmost request of another person.

There is a zen story about a Buddhist monk who was also an artist. He charged high prices for his artwork and always insisted on being paid in advance. To the unawakened mind it appeared that this monk was just as greedy and money-grabbing as the most selfish worldling. The monk was called the stingy artist. Years later, however, it was learned that all the money the stingy artist earned went to fulfill three demands of his inmost request: he built and filled a secret warehouse to help the poor people in his province survive famines; he built a better road from his village to the National Shrine; and he built a temple for his master, who had passed away before he was able to accomplish his own inmost request. After the stingy artist satisfied all the demands of his karmic nucleus, he gave up painting for profit and retired to live a simple life in the mountains.

Sometimes we are fortunate to be able to work in the light, or full knowledge, of our inmost request. But at other times we must be content to work in darkness or ignorance. In the case of the artist-monk, we do not know if he realized from the first why he was moved to accumulate so much money. Perhaps he only realized the true nature of his inmost request later on. It really doesn't matter, except to our ego, if we work in ignorance or work in enlightenment. Eventually our inmost request will be awakened and completely fulfilled—if not by us, then by one of our successors.

Sometimes the demands of our inmost request may appear crazy to the ordinary, unawakened mind. When St. Francis of Assisi first awakened his inmost request, he understood only a part of it. He was not yet ready to accept his full *karma*, which was to rekindle the spirit of the whole Christian world. It is the tendency of the religious spirit to fall asleep from time to time, and when it does, a great need is born in human form to reawaken itself. Lama Govinda, a contemporary Tibetan Buddhist sage, expresses the religious situation this way: "When religion grows in age, faith turns into dogma, and experience is replaced by book-knowledge, virtue by adherence to rules, devotion by ritual, meditation by metaphysical speculation. The time is then ripe for a rediscovery of truth and a fresh attempt to give it expression in life." At the time of St. Francis, the Christian religion had begun to grow old and stale, and the inmost request of the age and culture was to arouse the original spirit of Christianity.

At first, Francis interpreted his inmost request as a divine order to rebuild an old church in his neighborhood. Perhaps it was just as well that Francis didn't fully appreciate the magnitude of the task he had accepted. But even though Francis did not recognize the great extent of his inmost request he *did* recognize its great power. There is no questioning the power of our karmic nucleus once it is aroused.

Francis robbed his father in order to get the money to restore God's church. But his *karma* soon caught up with him and made it clear that the way to appease an inmost request is not to steal, or to borrow, but to beg. Out of the humiliation he experienced from being branded a thief, Francis aroused the spirit of his beggar's mind. He threw away his pride; he threw away his inheritance; he threw away his security; he cut himself off from his old hometown; and he began begging for his bare necessities—not just crusts of bread, but stones to rebuild the old church. Everyone thought he had lost his senses. Everyone except, perhaps, the stones with which St. Francis rebuilt the church. The stones must have known what later Christians found out, that the religious fool is not one that can be judged by ordinary standards.

Tenko-San, like St. Francis, Jesus, and Buddha, reawakened and cultivated the true spirit of religious begging. Tenko-San said that many people believe that it is impossible to engage in missionary work without money. He answered these skeptics by telling them that just the opposite is true; money hinders missionary work. He pointed out that work done by means of money is tainted by money; work done by means of power and position is tainted by power and position. True religion does not depend on money, or power, or position, or even intellectual knowledge. Tenko-San said a true religion is one in which a man with empty pockets is able to show others how to overcome suffering and find true freedom.

Religious begging, as it is ordinarily misunderstood, is an exchange. The monk begs from his neighbors for the bare necessities of life, and in return the neighbors receive a measure of good *karma*. In awakened begging there is nothing exchanged. When the zen beggar realizes that everything and everyone is Buddha-nature—that the enlightened and unenlightened, the sentient and insentient, are only projections of his own enlightenment or his own ignorance—then he knows that everyone from whom he begs is a projection of his own karmic nucleus. Awakened begging deepens and extends awareness. Whatever happens in our begging practice, whether we are helped or frustrated, we are skillfully directed by the innate power of our original nature deeper and deeper into the center of our zen environment. According to an old zen saying, "The Way is not difficult, just avoid picking and choosing." If this is true, then a beggar's life is the Way. Everyone knows beggars can't be choosers.

VII

Dropping Out

"There!"

"Where?" Jack asks, stopping the truck.

"To your left about a hundred yards up the side of the mountain." I point to a doe and a buck grazing in front of some chaparall.

"Yeah. I see them now," Jack whispers. "I told you this morning I smelled a deer, didn't I?" He reaches for his rifle.

"Your sense of smell is like an animal's," I whisper back.

"Like a mountain lion's when I'm hungry for meat." He quietly opens the truck door and leaves it ajar. He stands still for a few minutes. The deer watch him with interest but don't seem alarmed. Jack walks up the road slowly, then raises the rifle and fires.

Bam! The head of the buck jerks, and the body collapses and slides downhill about ten feet. The doe, startled by the noise, takes off up the hill but then stops and looks back, puzzled for a moment, before continuing slowly on over the ridge.

Jack bleeds the dead buck and drags it down to the truck. I help him lift it into the pickup. I notice that the bullet hit under the jaw and went out through an eye. There was no suffering.

Many Buddhists and nature lovers look down upon hunters who will kill an animal when moved by their *karma* to do so. Jack doesn't *love* nature. He respects it. He kills with awareness, appreciation, and skill. Jack has always been a hunter. It runs in his family. Not in mine. But I've lived with Jack long enough to learn to respect the hunter's spirit and to find deep traces of it in my own cultural background. The hunting spirit is a natural one that man shares with many other animals.

Jack believes in aiming for the head of the deer. That way, it's either a hit or a miss. There's little chance of wounding the animal and allowing it to get away to suffer a lingering death. One shot. Sudden and clean. As shocking as enlightenment.

I usually help Jack gut the carcass and skin it. I help him hang it and, when it's time, cut it up, cook it, and eat it. I've never shot a deer myself. Perhaps it isn't my *karma*. Or perhaps it isn't time yet. Someday, if Jack thrusts the gun in my hands and says, "Shoot!" I don't think I'll hesitate. I'll aim for the head. It will depend on the *karma* of the deer whether it will be a hit or a miss.

I was once a vegetarian. I didn't believe in killing and eating animals. But I gave up this practice when I discovered that my objection to not killing and eating animals was an attempt to escape the full realization of my own death. I didn't want to think about death. Death was too awful. I wanted to hang onto a childish fantasy: the belief that if I didn't kill or eat animals then I would escape being killed and eaten by death. I was attached to my personality and wanted it to continue forever.

This overemphasis on the sacredness of personal life doesn't satisfy me now. Death is also sacred. I want to be aware of my death as well as to be aware of my life. Perhaps it is only my childish fantasy, but I like to think of death as a skillful hunter. I don't want my death to be sentimental, or hesitant, or sloppy. When it is my time to die, I want to die quickly. Suddenly. I want death to bleed me, and gut me, and skin me, and hang me, and cut me up, and eat me. I want to be thoroughly digested by death and to be reborn in the spirit of Vast Emptiness.

Now, I'm not saying that it is always OK to kill animals and eat meat, or that it is always self-deceiving to practice nonviolence and vegetarianism. It's only the attachment to nonviolence and vegetarianism (and Zen Buddhism) that is self-deceiving. And, as you may remember, attachment is created when we think something is always good or always bad. I look at it this way: if you are a meat-eating deer, you are a neurotic deer. And if you are a vegetarian mountain lion, you are a neurotic mountain lion. When you know what you are, then you will be able to kill or not-kill, eat meat or not-eat meat without creating waves of karmic confusion. I might add that I've noticed, during the years that Jack and I have been together, he seems to be hunting less frequently and eating less meat. In his next life he may be a deer.

Disrupting the routines of life is a splendid phrase introduced by don Juan, the Yaqui Indian sage who is intuitively acquainted with the spirit of Rinzai's Man of No Title. When the sage first introduces his apprentice, Carlos Castaneda, to the importance of disrupting the routines of his life, don Juan uses the art of hunting as an example. But when don Juan speaks of hunting game, I don't think he means just ordinary hunting or ordinary game. The real prey of the apprentice, as well as the zen student, is knowledge (as don Juan calls it), or *bodhi* (as zen masters call it). Don Juan explains that a good hunter doesn't catch game just by setting traps or by knowing the habits of his prey; he succeeds because he doesn't have any predictable habits of his own. Don Juan points out that a hunter who has fixed habits behaves just like the animals he is hunting. Fixed habits make the hunter an easy prey himself. The good hunter must get rid of all of his fixed routines and habits so that he won't get trapped by other hunters. When we have predictable routines, we become the prey of our own ego and of the egos of other people. When we are liberated from the routines of our old hometown, we are able to catch the big game, knowledge or *bodhi*. The big game finally reveals itself where it has been hiding all along, under our own belt.

Learning about zen is a process of unlearning what we have learned all our lives. Going to a monastery, or practicing *zazen* with a zen master or a zen group, allows us to give our normal routines and habits a rest while we concentrate on some new ways. It is the old routines that tie us to our old hometown, to our ego, and to our limited image of ourself and the world. But in studying and practicing zen we must be careful not to let the new zen practices and attitudes become so routine that they turn into another old hometown. This is why a taste of the *unsui*, a monk's cloud-water life, is so important to the full understanding of zen.

In the past, zen monks often spent their cloud-water period traveling on foot to zen monasteries and temples in their native country of Japan. In this way they got a taste of zen practices different from the ones they had acquired from their own master. When zen was still flourishing in China, Japanese zen monks sometimes spent their cloud-water life wandering in China. Today American zen students are often encouraged by their zen teachers to go to Japan for a year or two of practice and study. After six to ten years of cultivating the zen environment, a zen student might consider taking another kind of practice trip. He might consider dropping out of Zen Buddhism for a year or two, refraining, during that time, from studying or practicing zen or associating with other Zen Buddhist practitioners.

The idea first came to me when a fellow zen student told me about a concert pianist he knew who studied many years with an excellent music teacher. After the teacher was satisfied that the student had acquired a mastery of the technique, he told the student to go into the woods and live alone for two years. During that time the piano student was not to touch a piano or listen to any music except the natural sounds in his environment. After that period was completed, the teacher said the student would be ready to prepare for his first concert.

Practicing zen and practicing music have something in common. I have heard people complain that the phrase "zen practice" turns them off. They want to experience the spontaneity of zen without practicing the scales of zen. But whether we like it or dislike it, practice is just as necessary to zen expression as it is to musical expression. On the other hand, practice tends to inhibit spontaneity and increase self-consciousness. Dropping out of zen practice for a period of a year or two is an excellent way to drop off our attachment to our training. After coming back from a no-practice trip, the zen student should be able to resume zen practice spontaneously and joyfully. And he should be in a better position to begin teaching others.

The environment in which the zen student takes his vacation from zen practice is important. It should be in an area quite different from his old hometown, but it should not be too close to the hometown of his zen master. If possible, the zen student should go to a place where no one knows anything about zen or Buddhism, and no one knows anything about the student. A foreign country might be the first choice. Each one of us has someplace that we dream of visiting someday. This may be the ideal environment for taking a no-zen vacation.

Of course, most of us will have to find some kind of work to support us during our no-practice trip. Very few of us have the time or money to take a year off from work. But it is not necessary to work at our usual job. In fact, it might be better to work at something out of our ordinary line. In this way we can take a vacation from our livelihood as well as from our zen practice. When I suddenly was moved by my *karma* to come to Big Sur, I didn't consciously plan to become a zen dropout. It happened quite spontaneously. A year and a half later I was moved, just as spontaneously, to resume zen practice. I returned from my vacation refreshed, relaxed, and with a much broader view of the zen environment. I had lost many of the attachments to Zen Buddhism that I had developed during the years of my training.

The most important thing in dropping out of zen—other than stopping all zen practice and study—is that the student should make no effort to teach or convert his neighbors. Of course, he won't succeed, but he should at least make the effort. And if he is an ordained Zen Buddhist he should pack away his robes during his vacation. The zen student should concentrate on opening his heart, and mind, and his whole body to the true nature of his environment. Like the concert pianist, he should listen to the sounds of original nature with all his senses. He should try humbly to accept everyone and everything in his environment as his special teacher.

By the time he resumes zen practice, the dropout zen

student's style should be unpredictable, much freer, and more fluid. Old Buddhas will have difficulty managing him. New Buddhas will try to become his intimate companions. Zen practice will no longer be routine but will arise spontaneously and develop creatively to suit the time, the place, and the occasion.

/

VIII

Cut It Off!

While I mend wool socks this afternoon, Jack sharpens and polishes his old double-bladed ax. I listen to the sound of steel on whetstone, hear a hawk screeching, look up now and then to watch the dry leaves of the oak tree flutter past the front window of the cabin. When Jack passes me to go outside, I smell the oil on his hands, and while he is gone, I touch the cool sharpness, feel the pain of the blade.

He glues and wraps the split end of the handle with black tape, stains the wood green, and then leans the ax against the cabin wall. He goes into the kitchen and returns with two glasses of wine. We drink our wine slowly, looking out the open door past the pine trees, listening to the whispering of homeless ghosts. The autumn evening deepens, and for some unknown reason I feel moved by melancholy.

How often we have said, or heard others say, "I'd give my right arm to..." meaning that we would give up something we cherish in order to receive something worth even more. Intuitively we all are acquainted with the profound nature of renunciation or sacrifice. The human path of material and spiritual liberation is a series of renunciations, from the first—giving up the bottle or the breast for the cup—to the last—giving up our body, mind, and earthly life for the sake of itself.

Shikan-taza zen practice is the way to bring the mature spirit of the final sacrifice into every aspect of our immature life. There are many zen stories emphasizing the enlightening practice of sacrifice. Perhaps the most well known and the most classic is the legend of Eka, the first disciple of Bodhidharma, who, it is said, *did* cut off his arm, offering it to the First Patriarch in exchange for the highest teaching of Buddhism.

Perhaps this is the place to stop and consider once again the notion of legends in general. The stories of Buddha, Bodhidharma, Hui-neng, Lao-tzu, Jesus, and other religious heroes are often discounted by those addicted to logical intellectual reasoning as primitive superstitions. We are often told that legends and myths are worthless because they are not historically factual. But even though legends, myths, fairy tales, and religious scriptures may have some connection with historical fact, they are not meant to be literal descriptions of everyday, logical reality. They depict, through narrative form, psychological and spiritual levels of reality.

It is as meaningless to discredit a legend because it does not represent logical truth as it would be to discredit a work of art because it does not closely resemble a photograph of the subject. A legend is like a *koan;* it is a mirror to hold up before our true nature. When we recognize ourselves in the mirror of a legend, we recognize an aspect of our inner nature. When we recognize ourself in the mirror of a *koan,* we recognize our original nature, the one we had before our ego was born.

Returning to the legend of Bodhidharma and Eka: the Indian Patriarch, having been moved by his *karma* to China, was invited by the devout Buddhist Emperor Wu to an audience at the palace in order to answer questions on Buddhism. When the Emperor asked Bodhidharma, "What is the highest truth of the holy Buddhist doctrine?" Bodhidharma answered, "Vast emptiness with not a trace of holiness, sire." The Emperor didn't understand. "If there is nothing holy," he asked Bodhidharma, "then who [what] are you?" Bodhidharma replied, "I don't know, sire."

After his audience with the Chinese Emperor, Bodhidharma settled down in Shao-lin Monastery where he sat in meditation nine years facing the great wall of the stubborn Chinese intellect. For nine years Bodhidharma's silent message penetrated deeper and deeper into the bedrock of Chinese conditioning. The *mudra* was the message. The highest truth of Buddhism was Bodhidharma, sitting alone, preaching to the stones in the great intellectual wall of China, waiting for it to crumble.

We can imagine many enthusiastic young Chinese Buddhists visiting Bodhidharma during the nine years that the Patriarch practiced wall gazing alone. We can be sure that many of them hoped to be accepted as disciples of the Patriarch. But none of these young intellects could move the Indian sage, that is, not until a middle-aged Confucian scholar, Eka, approached the master and asked for instruction. The sage remained sitting. Not realizing that Bodhidharma *was* giving him instruction, Eka stood for days in the snow, waiting for some verbal teaching from the Patriarch.

Finally, in complete frustration, Eka cut off his left arm with the sword he was carrying and offered it to Bodhidharma to show how sincerely he wished to receive the Buddhist teaching. Bodhidharma's compassion was touched by the great need of Eka's inmost request. The Patriarch turned around to recognize a possibility. "What do you want?" Bodhidharma roared, his eyes glowing like redhot coals and his beard hanging with icicles. "I want to be instructed in the doctrine of Buddhism," replied Eka, unwaveringly. Bodhidharma realized that Eka was not a man to be measured by ordinary standards. He told Eka that Buddhism could not be realized through someone else. Eka then roused his beggar's mind; he asked Bodhidharma to pacify his troubled soul (or self). Bodhidharma answered, "If you bring me your soul I will pacify it for you." Eka said, "I have searched for my soul for many years, but I am unable to grasp it." Bodhidharma announced, "There, it is pacified!"

We must remember that legends and *koans* are often very condensed, so we must try to read between the lines and fill in, by our own experience, what actually happened between the master and the disciple. It is quite likely that

when Bodhidharma announced: "There, it is pacified!"
that Eka was thrown into an intense concentration, or
what in zen is called the great doubt. (I spoke about this
earlier in my own experience.) It may have been months
before Eka was able to accept completely his true soul-less
or selfless nature. But when he finally realized that there
was nothing to be gained from Buddhism, that there was
no soul or self to seek, Eka's mind was set at rest. It was
pacified. It is said that Eka remained with Bodhidharma
nine more years, practicing *zazen* for the sake of itself.
When Bodhidharma returned to India, Eka became the
second zen patriarch of China, and I have read that he
lived the rest of his life among the poor.

There are two kinds of sacrifices in zen practice: those
that cut off our attachments to our old hometown (ego
attachments), and those that cut off our attachments to
our Buddha-nature (mythic attachments). The first kind
are immature sacrifices—giving up something for the sake
of something we imagine to be worth more. The second
kind are mature sacrifices—giving up something for nothing, for the sake of itself. Both kinds of sacrifices are the
results of long and frustrating battles between our image
of ourself and our real "self."

When Zen Buddhist monks become ordained, they shave
off all their hair. This kind of formal sacrifice, which
symbolically represents the cutting off of the monk's ego
attachments and his attachments to his worldly life, is an
example of the first kind of sacrifice. The monk gives up
his worldly personality and his worldly life for a religious
personality and a religious life—which he usually considers more valuable. But when a Zen Buddhist monk realizes that Buddha is the same as a worldly person, that the
religious life is no better than a worldly life, then the
monk is free to return to ordinary life as a *bodhisattva* (or to
remain in the religious life as a *bodhisattva*). This is an
example of the second kind of sacrifice.

There are other kinds of symbolic sacrifices that also
represent outer expressions of inner changes. One example of the first kind of sacrifice involves one of my *dharma*
brothers who was a talented cook. During his spare time

at Tassajara he collected recipes which he planned to publish in a book. This *dharma* brother came to me one day with a problem that had been troubling him for some time. He was torn between his desire to finish his cookbook and his desire to concentrate all his energy on his zen practice. He asked me if I thought he should abandon his cookbook project. Probably because I wanted a copy of his cookbook, I said I thought he should finish his book first, and then he'd be free to concentrate wholeheartedly on his meditation.

Some months later my *dharma* brother told me that he had thrown his unfinished cookbook in the incinerator. I was disappointed. He said that when he told Suzuki Roshi what he had done, Roshi had laughed and announced that it was time for him to go to Japan. Before he left, my *dharma* brother told me he planned to continue his practice of Zen Buddhism in Japan. He wanted to concentrate on learning the Japanese language because he hoped eventually to be able to make a new English translation of the works of Dogen Zenji. I haven't heard from him for years, but I appreciate now the importance of his sacrifice. It was necessary for him to cut off the right arm of the cook in order to arouse the right arm of his *bodhidharma* nature.

One of my own encounters with the phenomenon of sacrifice occurred during the period at Tassajara when I became possessed by the power I called the Hermit. (Earlier, you may remember, I used the legend of Buddha's birth to describe the temporary mythic inflation of that complex experience.) At that time I "cut off my tongue." I suddenly stopped talking one day and didn't speak again for eight months. Why? At the time I had no idea why. But in order not to appear crazy, I called it a vow of silence. Just as I did not really take the vow to save all sentient beings, I also did not really take the vow of silence. The vow took me.

Looking back, I realize the vow of silence was a reaction to my frustration over my inability to understand the nature of my "self." I might have saved myself a lot of grief if I hadn't tried to understand myself and instead had heeded Katagiri Roshi's warning that even if we reach the source of the river, we will never understand the totality of the river. But by trying to understand what is impossible to understand, we extend our understanding of ourselves—a little.

"Cutting off my tongue" was a spontaneous expression of the spiritual conflict symbolized by the Eka-Bodhidharma legend. In this legend Eka represents our ordinary ego, while Bodhidharma represents our original nature. Our ego carries a sword (a power) to cut off its arm (its attachment to itself). It is necessary to cut off our attachment to our ego before *bodhi* is awakened or, as it is expressed in the legend, before Bodhidharma "turns around."

The intimate relationship between our ego and some part of our body may have been recognized by Jesus when he said: "If thy right eye offend thee, cast it out..." During my eight months of silence I discovered, among other things, that my tongue was the member of my body most directly connected to my ego. Cutting off my tongue effectively cut off my strongest attachments to my old hometown. Later I read that Buckminster Fuller spent two years in silence, which was brought on by the frustrating limitations of verbal communication. When he began talking again, it was with a "redesigned instrument." I found that when I began talking again, it was with a redesigned image of my "self."

When Jack broke his leg, on the ninth anniversary of my first meeting with Suzuki Roshi, I asked myself later if there could be some connection between his accident and the nature of *bodhi-dharma*, or enlightenment teaching. And I discovered that the effect of Jack's involuntary sacrifice was similar to the effect of my own "voluntary" sacrifice. It cut off his ego attachment. Jack's legs, like my tongue, had been his means of escaping his karmic nucleus. His legs (and the extensions of his legs—his wheels) were the members of his body that always carried him back to his old hometown. Forced by his accident to sit still, Jack began to get to know himself, instead of being able to run away from himself.

I remember Suzuki Roshi recommending to one of his male disciples that he spend two years in celibacy. Roshi knew which member kept this student attached to his old hometown. Celibacy is an effective way to cut it off, but, because not all of us are troubled by the same attachments, zen monks are not all required to observe the religious vows of celibacy.

You always have to sacrifice something very dear to you before you can become a never-returner to your old hometown. So if it is your right eye, or right arm, or left leg, or your tongue, or your tail that ties you to your old image of yourself, *cut it off!* A zen student may have to cut off many things and many ideas before he finds the courage and the insight to cut off his most troublesome ego attachment, the attachment to Buddha. This is the mature sacrifice. He gives up Buddha for nothing but Bodhidharma's Vast Emptiness. But giving up something for nothing isn't the final sacrifice. There is still one more sacrifice to make. For it is the nature of *bodhi-dharma*, or zen teaching, to trap us in its Vast Emptiness. If it does— *cut it off!* The impact of cutting off the cutting off is like returning to our old hometown after a long journey. For the first time we are able to settle down where there is no settling down—in the real zen environment.

IX

Patchrobed Zen

Here in this humble mountain cabin on the east side of a great oak tree I sift the ashes of yesterday's dreams. This incense bowl is carved from the root of a yucca plant that lived and died on Marble Peak. The yucca is not a plant to be judged by ordinary standards. Like the lotus, the yucca is a Buddha teaching us the way to live and the way to die. Year after year, the homely yucca sits alone on the mountain, doing *shikantaza* up to the hilt. Year after year, it produces nothing but a clump of steel-gray, swordlike leaves. Then, after many years of meditation, the Buddha-nature of the plant is suddenly awakened. That spring it sends forth one sturdy stem, as tall as Shakyamuni and robed like a prince in a cluster of pale yellow flowers. Then, having realized itself completely, the yucca dies to its old life and is instantly transported to Mount Grdhrakuta where Buddha holds it aloft for everyone to see. Once again, the one who recognizes the true nature of an ordinary flower shows Buddha the smile lines on his original face.

I light a stick of pine incense and set it in the bowl. Soon the fresh fragrance fills the room and drifts through the cracks in the cabin walls. Suzuki Roshi told me that when we light incense it is an invitation to Buddha, who is passing by our house, to come in and sit with us. I open the windows of the cabin and invite the spirit of my old master to join me here in my small room.

I spread my grass mat on the rough floor and bow nine times. I set my *zafu* on the mat. I *gassho* to the one who is already sitting on my *zafu;* I turn and *gassho* to the one who is already sitting across the room. Then I sit down on the cushion and cross my legs.

My meditation cushion is made from scraps of discarded cotton material which I picked up here and there in my cloud-water life. The idea for a patchwork *zafu* came to me after reading about an incident in the life of Maha-Kasyapa, Gautama Buddha's successor.

Maha-Kasyapa was a very simple and humble man. Before he met Buddha, Maha-Kasyapa had a following of religious practitioners of his own, so his zen practice was rather mature. He was a forest dweller and a lover of solitude. He begged for alms and always wore cast-off clothing. Buddha was more polished in his zen expression than Maha-Kasyapa. You might say that Buddha's zen was as refined as silk, while Maha-Kasyapa's zen was as plain as cotton.

After becoming Buddha's disciple, Maha-Kasyapa must have felt a temptation to try to refine his zen practice so that it looked more like Buddha's. This is natural. When we are moved to become the disciple of a zen master, we usually want to become more like our master. But if we try to imitate our zen master, we will become nothing but an imitation. It takes most zen students years and years to find this out by experience. But Maha-Kasyapa realized this very quickly. It only took him seven days. He realized that even though his own life-style, personality, and expression of zen were different from Buddha's, underneath they were essentially the same.

Not long after this insight, Maha-Kasyapa had an opportunity to demonstrate his realization to Buddha—not in words, but more directly. As the two of them were out walking, Maha-Kasyapa saw Buddha turning off the road, and he knew intuitively that Buddha was planning to sit under a certain tree. Maha-Kasyapa folded his patched cotton robe to make a cushion and invited Buddha to sit on it under the tree. After meditating on Maha-Kasyapa's patched robe, Buddha said, "Friendly indeed, Kasyapa, is this patched cotton robe of yours. It is soft, of good texture, well made, and comfortable."

In praising Maha-Kasyapa's robe, Buddha was actually praising Maha-Kasyapa's zen practice. The Buddhist robe represents the *dharma*, or teaching, handed down from Buddha. The early followers of Gautama Buddha traditionally wore either a saffron-colored, hempen robe, like the garments worn by Indian criminals; or else they made robes out of scraps taken from dung heaps. After Buddha praised his disciple's patched robe, Maha-Kasyapa offered it to Buddha, and in return Buddha presented his own robe to Maha-Kasyapa.

This incident in the lives of Buddha and Maha-Kasyapa expresses very simply and clearly the original meaning of Zen Buddhist *dharma* transmission and ordination. Strictly speaking, Buddhist transmission is identical to Buddhist ordination. So the ordination ceremony should express the true spirit of full transmission.

Transmission isn't a complicated affair. It's very simple. Like friendship. True transmission, like true friendship, doesn't flow in one direction only, from the zen master to the zen student. It flows both ways simultaneously. Transmission is a mutual giving and mutual receiving. It is an identification between master and disciple, a realization of not two and not one.

One of my zen teachers, Kobun Chino Roshi, pointed out: "Transmission is not like passing old fancy furniture to the grandson. The job of the new generation is to create the tradition, to transmit the *spirit* of the tradition." Suzuki Roshi transmitted the spirit of the tradition on the first morning I met him (in this life). After meditating together, he said: "I can only teach you Japanese zen. In time you will find your own zen. First you must learn Japanese zen, and later you will discover American zen. You will be zen pioneers."

It was a simple message, but powerful. It pierced through my emotional armor and my intellectual straightjacket to settle deep in my guts. But it wasn't just a personal message. It was a special message, like the one the great zen pioneer, Bodhidharma, transmitted to his disciple Eka; or the message Buddha transmitted to his disciple Maha-Kasyapa. The spirit of a zen transmission is always the same. It is only the form that changes.

* * *

Both my first and second zen masters offered to ordain me as a Zen Buddhist priest. And both times I resisted. My *karma* would not allow me to be ordained as a Zen Buddhist priest, and it would not allow me to be ordained as a Zen Buddhist laywoman. I didn't exactly fit into either category.

Ordination as a Buddhist priest usually takes place before full transmission occurs. It corresponds with what I have described as the first phase of zen. Generally it is the first zen master who recognizes the Buddha-nature of the zen student and who ordains him as an *unsui*, or Zen Buddhist monk. In the ordination ceremony the monk receives a new name, a bowing mat, three robes, and a set of begging bowls. At this time the monk confesses and renounces past wrongdoing and vows to keep the Buddhist precepts.

The next rank of priesthood usually corresponds with what I have described as the second phase of zen. It is a period in which the chief junior monk engages in active practice teaching, generally at a Zen Buddhist temple or monastery. The ceremony performed at the time of entrance into this rank expresses the testing and challenging (*bodhi-dharma*) spirit of the second phase of zen.

The next rank of zen usually corresponds with what I have described as the third phase of zen. The transmission ceremony, generally performed in secret by the third, or true master, expresses the monk's graduation into full priesthood.

To be offered Buddha's robe, not just once but twice, and to refuse it, not just once but twice, is not a matter to be taken lightly. Dogen Zenji was very strict on this matter. He went so far as to say, in an essay on the merit of wearing the Buddhist robe, that the attitude of those who have realized their Buddha-nature and yet refused to accept the Buddha's robe was "unpardonable, due entirely to their extreme foolishness and unbelief."

This may be true, but not always. Since ordination is the same as transmission (much as two sides of one coin are the same as each other, but not exactly), it is obvious that if ordination occurs, sooner or later transmission will manifest itself. Or if transmission occurs, then sooner or later ordination will manifest itself. It depends on *karma*, however, just how long it will take for the flip side of the coin to appear. While most disciples receive ordination before transmission, or shortly after, this is not always the case. The sixth zen patriarch, Hui-neng, for example, waited fifteen years after he had secretly received true transmission from the Fifth Patriarch before he came out of seclusion and was formally ordained into the Buddhist order. He spent those fifteen years living in the mountains. To his neighbors he appeared to be just an ordinary man, but, unknown to them, he was practicing *shikan-taza* up to the hilt—extending and deepening his zen transmission.

When I was at Tassajara, Suzuki Roshi once asked me to think about a new design for a Buddhist robe that would clearly manifest the true spirit of American Zen Buddhism. Roshi realized the difference between American zen and Japanese zen. He said once: "Here in America we cannot define Zen Buddhists the same way we do in Japan. American students are not priests and yet not completely laymen. I understand it this way; that you are not priests is an easy matter, but that you are not exactly laymen is more difficult. I think you are special people and want some special practice that is not exactly priest's practice and not exactly laymen's practice."

The "special" people Suzuki Roshi found in America are really not special at all. They are Maitreya Zen Buddhists. At the moment, Maitreya Zen Buddhism may appear to be revolutionary, but this is only in comparison with the traditional Buddhism of the past. When Bodhidharma Buddhism was being developed in China it, too, seemed revolutionary in comparison with the Shakyamuni Buddhism of India.

I personally feel that Maitreya Buddha wants a robe that will express his-her informal, democratic, pioneer spirit. And I feel that Maitreya Buddha also wants an ordination ceremony that is a mutual transmission of *dharma* robes, not only between two Buddhas, but between two old friends. So before the zen master offers the disciple the silk robe that represents the refined spirit of Japanese zen, the disciple might ask the master to meditate on the patched cotton robe that represents the crude spirit of American zen.

"Come Buddha, please sit for a while under this shadowless tree and meditate on my ragged, hand-me-down zen *dharma*. I have patched it together from scraps of material gathered from the garbage dumps of my zen environment. This patchwork *dharma* may look like a raggle-taggle affair, full of intellectual holes, but I think you will find it soft, of good texture, well made and comfortable."

Dogen Zenji pointed out that the materials for making a Buddhist robe may be either silk, cotton, or, if these are unavailable, other materials. He said that cotton was not necessarily pure, nor was silk necessarily impure. In other words, according to Dogen Zenji, we shouldn't discriminate between pure and impure, fancy or plain, silk or cotton. But then Dogen went on to discriminate (an annoying habit zen masters have) and said that the *best* material for a Buddhist robe is discarded cloth, preferably cloth that has been thrown away in the garbage dump.

Dogen twice refused to accept an honorary purple outer-robe offered to him by the Emperor of Japan. The third time the Emperor offered it to him, Dogen accepted the robe. But he vowed never to wear it during his lifetime. He wrote this poem to explain his "unpardonable" refusal:

> Shallow is the valley of Eiheiji temple,
> But grave is the edict of the emperor.
> If an old monk here wore a purple kasaya [outer-robe]
> He would be laughed at by monkeys and cranes.

Perhaps the material that best represents the democratic pioneer spirit of American Zen Buddhism is faded blue denim. Not only is this material worn by working people as well as prisoners in American jails, but it has become increasingly popular with all kinds and classes of Americans, women as well as men. So I am wondering if Maitreya Buddha might like a robe made out of pieces of cloth cut from discarded Levi's. How do you feel about it?

I've been meditating for many years on this matter of Buddhist ordination. Lately I've come to see both sides of the mountain. According to some interpretations, a *bodhi-sattva* is one who first enlightens himself and then helps enlighten others. But according to Dogen Zenji, the *bodhi-sattva* is one who helps everyone else attain enlightenment before he himself attains it. So a zen student who vows to postpone Buddhist ordination until all sentient beings are ordained is no different from a zen priest who wears Buddhist robes.

Suzuki Roshi told his beginning zen students that anyone of them who reverently recited the short poem chanted by zen monks after *zazen* would wear a Buddhist robe identical to his own. Since my old master taught me this, I believe it to be true. So for those, like myself, who don't yet wear the Buddhist robes but who wish to transmit the spirit of Buddhism forever, even if only to one true *bodhi* seeker, I suggest that after you have come to the end of a period of *zazen* you put your hands together in the *mudra* of *gassho* and reverently chant this *gatha* (*dharma* poem). The form of this robe *gatha* is not exactly the same as the one given to me by my master, but in essence it does not differ from the original, for both of them seep and trickle out of the same deep source—the compassionate heart of Buddha.

> *How wonderful to wear Shakyamuni's robe:*
> *Formless but embracing all form.*
> *Now as the* dharma *is unfolded*
> *May all sentient beings awaken.*
>
> *How wonderful to wear Bodhidharma's robe:*
> *Timeless but embracing all time.*
> *Now as the* dharma *is unfolded*
> *May all sentient beings awaken.*
>
> *How wonderful to wear Maitreya's robe:*
> *Uncreated but embracing all creation.*
> *Now as the* dharma *is unfolded*
> *May all sentient beings awaken.*

There is nothing left to do now but to sway back and forth a few times, unfold our *dharma* legs, and allow our *dharma* body to rise from its seat under the Bodhi Tree. If we follow our *dharma* feet, we will find ourselves once again walking along the road that leads from *bodhi* to Benares.

X

White Mountain

Yesterday it began to snow on Marble Peak. Today the snow is about a foot deep. It's warmer than usual inside the cabin because of the insulating layer of snow on the roof. I am reminded of a poem written by Dogen Zenji near the end of his life:

> Nothing in my life has left
>   a trace of the Path;
> My way lost between the true
>   and the false.
> For long days the snow has
>   covered the mountain;
> This winter it's the snow that
>   makes the mountain.

When we begin to appreciate that it's the difficulties and inconveniences that make our life, we begin to appreciate zen. Zen, like a layer of snow on the roof, insulates and warms our true nature. It is very difficult to explain the insulating comfort of zen to someone who has not experienced this way of life. My mother wrote me the other day and asked if Jack and I expected to settle here on Marble Peak. It seems to her that we put in so much work on all the places we have lived but always move on before we are able to enjoy the ripe fruits of our labor.

It is natural for my mother to doubt the value of this kind of life. From the ordinary point of view, our zen life leaves no trace of anything worthwhile. We have nothing to show for it, nothing to give from it, and nothing to say about it. Whatever we show, give, or say about it really isn't it.

When I try to answer the genuine concern of my mother, I find my way lost between the true and the false. For many years the snow has covered the mountain of my zen life. Compared to the lush fruits of the comfortable life that I was living before I began zen practice, my present life appears utterly destitute. Today, with the snow covering Marble Peak, and a mountain of failures covering my zen life, I feel some harmony between my inner and outer environments. This winter, too, it's the snow that makes the mountain.

I have no answer to give my mother which would pacify her troubled soul. I wish that I could tell her that I expect to settle down on Marble Peak because I have finally found the right environment. But even after we find the right environment, we cannot rest assured that we will be able to stay there. It depends on our *karma*. Samsara, our trailer home, is temporarily pastured in a spacious field, but we keep it stocked and ready to move.

From the front window of the cabin I can see the oak tree in the garden. It is leafless and laden with snow. But like the Buddhist goddess of compassion, Avalokitesvara, with her thousand arms, the oak tree reaches out to help all sentient beings. In summer it gives shade to the weary travelers, and in winter it gives its right arms to keep them warm. Last night a branch of the oak tree fell off, and this evening I threw it on the fire. It burns as brightly as a wooden Buddha.

It would be easy to become attached to the oak tree. When I look at it tonight, in the moonlight, I feel moved by my wood tick *karma* to hang onto it for dear life. It would be pleasant to settle down. But I remember the words of my zen master: "We must have beginner's mind, free from possessing anything, a mind that knows everything is in flowing change. Nothing exists but momentarily in its present form and color. One thing flows into another and cannot be grasped. Before the rain stops we hear a bird. Even under heavy snow we see snowdrops and some new growth. In the East I saw rhubarb already. In Japan in the spring we eat cucumbers."

A wind sweeps through the trees behind the cabin. The sound is enough to awaken the whole world from its dreams of childhood. Tonight we may make our home in this zen environment, surrounded by marble peaks and looking down into lost valleys, while an immense sheet of shining water stretches beyond the horizon. But tomorrow we may drift along with the snow that wraps the world in white. Forever to travel is our destiny, through a dream world of echoes and shadows.

This tattered life is my only robe; the wind my only refuge. It was here a moment ago, but already it has blown away.

Epilogue

Nine months later, on the first day of August 1977, a bolt of lightning struck a tree on the east side of Marble Peak and set the torch to one hundred seventy-five thousand acres of wilderness between Big Sur and Tassajara.

We sat through the conflagration that marked the end of a life. We felt the earth shake with the rumble of huge dozers, trucks, and tankers; we heard the valleys echo with the shouts of weary fire fighters; we saw the trees explode; we watched red glory-juice trailing in the wake of diving bombers, and we slept near black fingers of burned pines that pointed to blood-red moons. Before the fire was extinguished, a vast forest of tangled illusions was reduced to ash. But Tassajara and the oak tree on Marble Peak survived, like *saira* (sacred relics found in the ashes of a cremated Buddha).

Now, seven weeks after the sudden interruption to our peaceful meditation, the ground has finally cooled, and we are leaving. (The cabin we have been caretaking on Marble Peak has been sold.) We're on the road again. Living in our only permanent home, a tiny trailer I call Samsara. I'm thinking of what Kobun Chino Roshi said once: "Immediately after you stand on the peak of a mountain you step forward and begin to climb a higher mountain which is down below."

To the east, as far as I can see, the mountains are as blue-black as Bodhidharma's robe. To the west, where the fire didn't burn, a rounded ridge covered with wild oats inclines, like the golden shoulder of Buddha, toward the shining ocean of peace. I have no feeling of regret today, leaving the oak tree behind. I have only the feeling of certainty that no matter how far I will travel in this dream called life, it will be impossible to find a time or place that is not shaded by its cool wisdom. The tree on Marble Peak was a temporary manifestation of . . .

"Jack!"

"Look at that rack!"

Unmoved by the sound of our old brown truck chug-a-lugging down the dusty mountain road—a huge buck, close as reaching out and touching. Three bends on, looking back, I see him still standing his ground, his does grazing his gentle slopes, his hawks circling his cloudless sky, his ships sailing his endless ocean, and you and I traveling, traveling—never arriving at the end of his golden pasture.

Gassho

With palms together I wish to express my sincere gratitude by bowing in four directions:

First, to the direction of my parents, who claim they don't know anything about zen or Buddhism, but who express the *bodhisattva* spirit in their everyday life;

Second, to the direction of the many other *bodhisattvas* (disguised as ordinary people) who gave me food, clothes, books, lodgings, typewriters, typing paper, and good counseling—things I needed to satisfy a part of my inmost request;

Third, to the direction of my Buddhist teachers and friends, who read the manuscript in different stages and gave me many valuable suggestions: Taisan Maezumi Roshi, director of Zen Center of Los Angeles, California; Kobun Chino Otogawa Roshi, director of Bodhi in Los Altos, California; Dainin Katagiri Roshi, director of the Minnesota Zen Meditation Center; Dr. Eric Storlie, Barbara Heistand, Nancy James, Frances Thompson, and Pam (Yuko) Conniff-Hagen; who caught some of my mistakes but are not responsible for any others I might have made;

Fourth, to the direction of my husband, Jack, who never once read the manuscript and who doesn't intend to because he says he wouldn't understand it even if he could read it. Without Jack's skillful opposition, which roused my rebel spirit, I would have abandoned this middle-sized raft in the center of the Sea of Samsara.

Glossary

The following abbreviations are used:
Ch	Chinese
Jap	Japanese
Skt	Sanskrit
P	Pali

Agni (Skt). The ancient Indian god or spirit of fire.

Amida-butsu (Jap) **Amitābha** (Skt). Buddha of Infinite Light or Amitāyus (Skt) Buddha of Immeasurable Life. According to popular Buddhist belief, Amida Buddha resides in the Western Paradise, Pure Land, or Land of Bliss. A world savior who made a vow that he would refuse enlightenment for himself unless he could bring all who sincerely called upon his name to join him in his Pure Land. (See also Jōdō and Shin.)

anātman (Skt) **anattā** (P) **muga** (Jap). Gautama Buddha's doctrine of no-self or no-soul. That is, no personal, immortal, or substantial soul or self that transmigrates after death to another body. One of the Three Marks or Signs of Being in Buddhism.

anitya (Skt) **anicca** (P) **mujō** (Jap). Change. Transience. Impermanence. Gautama Buddha's doctrine that teaches that all things are impermanent and subject to change. One of the Three Marks or Signs of Being in Buddhism.

apratisthā (Ski) **mujū** (Jap). No-abode. Non-attachment. Literally, according to D. T. Suzuki, "not to have any home where one can settle down," but meaning actually "to settle down where there is no settling down" (in homelessness, emptiness, or transience).

ātman (Skt) **attā** (P) **ga** (Jap). The Brahman concept of self or soul. Popularly believed, in Buddha's day as well as our own, to be a personal soul, or dweller in the physical body, which never dies but transmigrates from life to life and can be joined in union with the universal self.

Aum (Skt). (See *Om*.)

Avalokiteśvara (Skt) **Kanzeon** or **Kannon** (Jap). The *bodhisattva* of Compassion. Literally "hearing the calls of suffering beings." Often represented with one thousand arms. (See also *bodhisattva*.)

Baker Rōshi. (See Zentatsu Baker Rōshi.)

Bashō (1643–1694). Japanese founder of the modern school of *haiku* poetry. *Bashō* means literally "banana plant." (See also *haiku*.)

bodhi (Skt) **bodai** (Jap). Perfect wisdom. Awakening. Enlightenment. Innate wisdom of everything. The mind that is free from ignorance and passions.

Bodhi. (See Haiku Zendo Foundation.)

Bodhidharma (Skt) **Bodai-daruma** (Jap) **P'u-t'i-ta-mo** (Ch) (died 528 or 536). The twenty-eighth Indian Buddhist patriarch and the first Chinese zen patriarch. Bodhidharma means literally "enlightenment teaching." Bodhidharma is said to have sat in meditation nine years facing a wall in Shorin-ji Temple in China. (See also *pi-kuan*.)

bodhisattva (Skt) **bosatsu** (Jap). Literally "enlightened being." A sage destined for enlightenment who seeks it not only for himself but for all others, or an enlightened sage who returns to the realm of ordinary beings to help them realize enlightenment.

Bodhi Tree (Skt) The tree under which Gautama Buddha became enlightened near Bodh Gayā in India. A pipal tree (*Fiscus religiosa*). Sometimes called the *Bo* Tree.

bonsai (Jap). The Japanese art of creating miniature trees.

Brahman (Skt) **Bon** (Jap). Literally "that which makes great." Divine ground of the universe in non-Buddhist Indian philosophy. Absolute and ultimate reality, on which everything else is only a manifestation.

brāhman (Skt). The name of the priest caste in India.

Buddha (Skt and P) **Butsu-da** (Jap). From the Sanskrit verb *budh*, which means "to know" or "to wake up." One who has awakened, cast off illusions. An enlightened one who is aware of the Truth. (See also Gautama Buddha and Shakyamuni.)

Buddha-Gayā (Skt). The site of Gautama Buddha's enlightenment in India. At the time of Buddha it was called Uruvela.

Buddha-nature Buddhatā (Skt) **Busshō** (Jap). The awakening or enlightenment nature of everything, not just human beings.

Burmese posture. A sitting posture used in meditation in which the legs are folded, one foot in front of the other, instead of one foot on top of the other thigh, as in the lotus posture. (See also lotus posture.)

Chino Rōshi (Kobun Chino Otogawa). Director of Haiku Zendo Foundation (now Bodhi) in Los Altos, California. He was first invited by Marian Mountain and Shunryu Suzuki Rōshi to come to Los Altos from Japan in 1967, but it was not until 1970 that he was able to assume full responsibility for the Los Altos zen group. He lives in Los

Altos with his American wife and two children. A close friend and teacher of Marian Mountain. (See also Haiku Zendo Foundation.)

City of Illusion. A metaphor from the *Lotus Sutra* which refers to false enlightenment.

cosmic mūdra (Skt). The hand position taken during *zazen* which is favored by the Sōtō School of Zen Buddhism.

dharma (Skt) **dhamma** (P) **hō** (Jap). A Buddhist teaching or doctrine. The law or order of the universe. Duty, right behavior, or virtue. A real event (as contrasted with a commonsense event). An attribute. A basic element of existence which is a force rather than a substance.

Diamond Sūtra. Sometimes called *Diamond Cutter Sūtra.* A small book which is part of the *Maha-Prajñā Paramitā* Scriptures of Buddhism. (See also *sūtra.*)

Dōgen Zenji (Kigen Dōgen). (1200–1253). Founder of the Sōtō Zen School in Japan. Many of his writings have been translated into English. (See also Eiheiji and *Genjo-Kōan.*)

dukkha (Skt). Usually translated as "ill" or "suffering" but may be closer to the idea of "frustration," "disappointment," or "imperfection." The first of the Four Noble Truths and one of the Three Marks or Signs of Being.

Eightfold Path. (See Noble Eightfold Path of Right Living.)

Eiheiji (Jap). Temple of Eternal Peace. One of the two head training monasteries of the Sōtō Zen School in Japan. Founded in the thirteenth century by Dōgen Zenji. (See also Dōgen Zenji.)

Eka (Jap) **Hui-k'ê** (Ch) (487–593). Second Chinese Zen Buddhist patriarch of China.

Emptiness. (See *śūnyatā.*)

Esalen Institute of Big Sur. Seminars on a wide range of subjects, such as psychology, science, education, religion, occult phenomena, meditation, and massage, are given by experts from all over the world. The magnificent setting and the natural hot springs make Esalen an ideal environment for expanding human consciousness.

Feng, Gia-fu (Ch). A contemporary Taoist sage, author, and *tai-chi* (meditative movements) teacher; a close friend and teacher of Marian Mountain when she was living in Los Altos. Now living and teaching at Stillpoint Foundation in Manitou Springs, Colorado.

Finger pointing to the moon. A phrase from *The Sūtra of the Perfect Awakening* which points out that all doctrines taught by Buddha must be understood only as "fingers pointing to the moon." They are tools, not real things.

gasshō (Jap). Palms together. The ancient Indian salutation. A gesture of gratitude, respect, and greeting.

Gateless Gate (*Mumon-kan*) (Jap). Literally "no gate barrier." A collection of forty-eight *kōans* compiled by the Chinese zen master Ekai who is usually known as Mumon. (See also *kōan* and Mumon.)

gatha (Skt) **ge** (Jap). A short verse praising Buddha or expressing Buddhist teaching.

Gautama Buddha (Skt) **Gotama Buddha** (P) (Siddhartha Gautama) (Skt). The historic Buddha who was born in India about 563 B.C. Gautama is not really the surname, but is the name of the clan in which Siddhartha was born. (See also Buddha and Shakyamuni.)

"Genjo-Koan" (Jap). An essay from the *Shōbō-genzo (Treasury of the True Teaching)* by Dōgen Zenji. (See also Dōgen Zenji and *kōan*.)

Golden-haired lion. A symbol for a person who is complete, full of virility, wholehearted, and expresses the whole truth.

Grdhrakuta, Mount (Skt). The place where Buddha first announced publicly that Mahā-Kāśyapa would be his successor.

guru (Skt). A spiritual guide in India. A religious teacher who takes disciples.

gyōun-ryūsui (Jap). Literally "floating clouds, running water" from which the Japanese name for zen monk *(unsui)* originates.

haiku (Jap). A seventeen-syllable poem which expresses an intuitive flash of enlightenment.

Haiku An (Jap). Haiku Temple. Specifically the *zendō* designed by Suzuki Rōshi and built by zen students in 1966 in the home of Marian Mountain in Los Altos. It seated about seventeen people. (See also *haiku* and *zendō*.)

Haiku Zendō Foundation. An incorporation of zen students who practiced meditation in Los Altos, California, under the guidance of Suzuki Rōshi, beginning in 1964. When Kobun Chino Rōshi became the group's full-time zen master in 1970, the name was changed to Bodhi. (P. O. Box 638, Los Altos, Ca.). In 1979 Bodhi purchased a church in Mountain View, California, which they converted to a Zen Buddhist Temple. Bodhi also has *zendōs* (or branches) in Saratoga, Ca., and Santa Cruz, Ca., among others. (See also Haiku An and Chino, Kobun.)

Han-shan (Ch) **Kanzan** (Jap). An eccentric hermit-poet who lived about 627–650 in China. His name means "cold mountain" and comes from the place where he lived.

hara (Jap). The solar plexus. The center of the body-mind, as well as the center of the whole universe in Buddhism.

Huang Po (Ch) **Ōbaku** (Jap) (Died 850). A famous Chinese zen master. Third in direct line of descent from the Sixth Chinese zen patriarch, Hui-nêng. Zen master of Linchi (Rinzai). His posthumous name is taken from Mount Huang Po where he resided for many years. His teachings have been preserved and have been translated into English. (See also Rinzai and Hui-nêng.)

Hui-nêng or **Wei-lang** (Ch) **Enō** (Jap) (638–713). The most famous zen master of the Tang dynasty. The sixth Chinese zen patriarch. An illiterate woodcutter who became enlightened after hearing a verse from the *Diamond Sūtra*. He was chosen as successor by his zen master, Hung-yen, the fifth Chinese zen patriarch, but suffered persecution for many years because of the jealousy of more erudite monks. His sermons have been preserved and translated into English, under the title of *The Platform Sūtra on the Treasury of the Law*. (See also *sūtra*, *Diamond Sūtra*, and *Sūtra of Hui-nêing*.)

Hung-yên (Ch) **Gunin** (Jap). The fifth zen patriarch of China.

I-Ching (Ch). *Book of Changes*. A collection of oracles based on the ancient Chinese mythic view of the universe.

Ittoen (Jap). Literally "The Garden of the One Light." A way of life featuring homelessness, poverty, and selfless service which was founded by Tenko Nishida in Kyoto, Japan, in 1913. See also Tenko-San.)

Jōdo-shū (Jap) **Ching-t'u** (Ch). The Pure Land school of Buddhism which originated in China and later developed into the Shin school. It features faith and good works. (See also Shin and Shinran.)

Jōshu (Jap) **Ch'ao-chou** (Ch) (778–897). A great zen master of the Tang dynasty. He is famous for his *kōans*, especially the *kōan* of *Mu*. Jōshu began the study of zen when he was sixty, realized enlightenment at eighty, and taught, it is said, until he was one hundred twenty years old. (See also *kōan* and *Mu*.)

kalavinka (Skt). A mythical Indian bird whose beautiful song can be heard even while it is still in the egg.

kalpa (Skt). An incalculable period of time. A mythological period of time.

karmic nucleus. The original nature of all Buddhists.

karma (Skt) **go** (Jap). Work or a deed. Effect of a deed. Law of action and reaction. Network of casual relationships governing mental and spiritual realms as well as the physical realm. In popular Buddhism it is believed that the conditions of our present life are due to our good or bad actions in a previous life. But Zen Buddhists do not believe in an entity or self that transmigrates from life to life, reaping the harvest of good and evil deeds. Karmic reactions are what are passed on from life to life.

kaṣāya (Skt) **kesa** (Jap). The rectangular Zen Buddhist outer-robe made of strips of cloth in different sizes and colors. It is draped over the under-robes and fastened at the left shoulder or carried folded over the left arm.

Katagiri Rōshi (Dainin Katagiri Rōshi). Close friend and teacher of Marian Mountain when he was teaching under Suzuki Rōshi from 1964 to 1972. Now practicing and teaching as director of the Minnesota Zen Meditation Center. (3343 E. Calhoun Parkway, Minneapolis, MN 55408.)

Kaye, Lester. Second lay director of Haiku Zendo Foundation. In 1968 the Kaye family moved into the "parsonage." Les and his wife Mary not only took over Marian Mountain's administrative duties, but also acted for a time as foster parents to two of Marian's teen-age children. In 1971 Les Kaye was ordained as a Zen Buddhist monk by Suzuki Rōshi. (See also Haiku An and Haiku Zendō Foundation.)

Kitano Gempo (Jap) (1841–1933). Abbot of Eiheiji Temple, one of the head temples of the Sōtō zen school of Japan. (See also Eiheiji.)

kōan (Jap) **kung-an** (Ch). Literally "public document." No-sense questions or statements. Meditation themes. Catalysts used to awaken zen students to their true nature and to test the genuineness of enlightenment. Used principally in the Rinzai zen school. (See also Rinzai.)

kyōsaku (Jap). "Awakening stick" carried by a monitor in the *zendō*, or meditation hall, which is used to hit meditating students on the shoulders to help them stay awake and to relieve stiffness. Sometimes called "Mañjuśurī's sword" which cuts off illusions. In the Rinzai zen school it is called *keisaku*, "policing stick," but is not used as punishment, only encouragement. (See also Mañjuśurī.)

Lama (Ch). Superior One. The title given to a fully ordained priest of Tibetan Buddhism.

Lao-tzu (Ch) (Born 604 B.C.). A legendary Chinese sage whose wisdom has been preserved in a famous Chinese classic, *Tao Teh Ching*. *Tao* means the way of all life; *teh* means the fit use of life by men; *ching* is text or classic.

lotus posture. The traditional sitting posture of zen meditation which originated in the school of Yoga. In the full lotus posture the legs are folded and crossed, with each each foot placed on the top of the opposite thigh. In the half-lotus posture only one foot is placed on the opposite thigh. (See also Yoga.)

Lumbini Gardens. The place in Nepal just over the Indian border where Siddhartha Gautama was born.

Mahā-Kāśyapa (Skt) **Maka-kasho** (Jap). The second Indian Zen Buddhist patriarch. One of the ten great disciples of Gautama Buddha.

makyo (Jap). Obstructions to meditation. Hallucinations or delusions. Strange physical and mental states which disappear when body and mind are fully harmonized.

Maitreya (Skt) **Miroku** (Jap). The future Buddha or the Buddha to come who, according to popular Buddhism, is now waiting in the Tusita heaven and is supposed to be born in human form about 2,500 years from now. In Zen Buddhism, Maitreya Buddha is our own innate Buddha-potential waiting to be awakened. Maitreya is derived from the Sanskrit word *maitrī*, meaning friendliness.

Maezumi Rōshi (Taizan Maezumi Rōshi). Director of the Zen Center of Los Angeles. (927 Normandie Ave., Los Angeles, California)

mandala (Skt). A mystical round picture used as an aid to meditation.

Mañjuśurī (Skt) **Monju** (Jap). A great *bodhisattva* of meditation who personifies wisdom. The name means literally "deep virtue" or "great fortune." He is usually shown riding on a lion and carrying, in one hand, a sword to cut away illusion, and in the other hand, a *sūtra*. (See also *kyōsaku*.)

Man of No Title, or **True Man of No Rank** *mui-no-shinnin* (Jap). A phrase used by the zen master Rinzai (Linchi) to point out our true nature or Buddha-nature. (See also Rinzai.)

mantra (Skt) **shingon** (Jap). A short mystical word or phrase which is spoken over and over, silently or out loud, and is believed to have the power to awaken or deepen spiritual awareness. Long mystical phrases are called *dhāranī* in Sanskrit.

Māra (Skt). The spirit of evil or death. The great tempter. The king of hell. A projection of our own shadow or negative side.

Middle Way *Chūdō* (Jap). The path or program outlined by Gautama Buddha as his answer to the problem of *dukkha*, or human frustration and disappointment, or suffering. It is popularly misunderstood as the happy medium between the extremes of sensuality and asceticism, or a synthesis between opposing concepts, such as good and evil; but according to Zen Buddhism, the Middle Way is a way which transcends all concepts.

mondo (Jap). Zen questions and answers.

Mu (Jap) **Wu** (Ch). Literally the negative symbol meaning "no" or "nothing." The name of the most famous *kōan* which is often given to beginning zen students. Like many *kōans* it is very short:

>   A monk asked Jōshu: "Has a dog Buddha-nature or not?"
>   Jōshu answered: "Mu."

Jōshu's *Mu* is considered the gate for the whole school of Zen Buddhism. *Mu* is not to be undertood intellectually but experienced directly. (See also *kōan, Gateless Gate,* and Jōshu.)

mūdra (Skt) **inzō** (Jap). A ritual gesture or posture, believed to have magical or mystical power.

Mumon Rōshi (Yamada Mumon Rōshi). Abbot of several zen temples in Japan and one of the most widely known and respected zen priests in Japan. He frequently visits zen centers in the United States.

Mumon (Mumon Ekai) (Jap) **Wu-mên Hui-k'ai** (Ch) (1183–1260). The Chinese zen master who made a collection of *kōans* called *Mumon-kan*. (See also *Gateless Gate* and *kōan*.)

Namu Amida Butsu (Jap). Literally "I put my trust in Amida Buddha." The Shin Buddhist *nembutsu* (to invoke the name of the Buddha) which is recited as a form of concentrated prayer to assist the true believer to attain enlightenment or salvation. (See also Amida, Shin, and Shinran.)

nirvāna (Skt) **nibbāna** (P) **nehan** (Jap). Literally "to blow out" or "to extinguish." A state of balance between body, mind, and *karma*. A condition where no illusions remain, and all the strong passions have cooled. Freedom from ignorance. The goal of Buddhist life.

Nishida, Tenko. (See Tenko-San.)

Noble Eightfold Path of Right (Perfect) Living. Buddha's prescription for liberation from *dukkha* (suffering). The steps are: right thought (or belief); right intention (or motives); right speech; right action; right livelihood; right effort; right mindfulness; and right meditation (or concentration). (See also *dukkha*.)

nyoi (Jap) **cinta** (Skt). A short staff carried by a zen master as a symbol of his teaching authority. A *nyoi* is not just a symbol but is the actualization of the power of the mythical *nyoi* jewel which the zen master gets from the Dragon-King of the sea (his karmic nucleus). (See karmic nucleus.)

old hometown. A phrase which is used symbolically in the book to represent the ordinary mind or the conditioned mind.

Om or **Aum** (Skt). A sacred sound used as a *mantra* by non-Buddhist Indians. The nameless Absolute. (See also *mantra*.)

Otogawa, Kobun Chino. (See Chino, Kobun.)

P'ang Chu-shi (Ch) **Ho-koji** (Jap) (740–803). A famous Chinese Buddhist layman and poet who threw all his material possessions into a river and lived a life of poverty thereafter.

Perls, Dr. Frederick (1893–1970). Gestalt psychiatrist, author, and resident teacher at Esalen Institute in Big Sur, California, for many years.

pi-kuan (Ch) **mempeki** (Jap). "Wall-gazing" or "wall-contemplation." The physical practice of facing the wall during meditation which may have begun with Bodhidharma, the first Chinese zen patriarch. The phrase also refers to a state of mind. (See also Bodhidharma.)

Pipal Tree. (See Bodhi Tree.)

Pure Land. (See Shin.)

Rinzai Gigen (Jap) **Linchi I-hsüan** (Ch) (died 867). A disciple of Huang-Po who founded the Rinzai zen school. Many of his writings have been translated into English.

rōshi (Jap). Respected master. Zen master. The term has the association of noble, old, and useless. This "uselessness," however, is something that transcends our ordinary concept of usefulness and uselessness.

Ryōkan (1758–1831). A poor zen master of the Sōtō zen school who lived alone in a small hut. He is loved by the Japanese people because of his zen poetry and his simple but profound zen spirit.

samsāra (Skt) **rinne** (Jap). Literally "becoming." Transmigration. The world as seen and experienced through ordinary conditioning. The endless round of birth and death. Moving about in circles. The rat race or squirrel cage. The Sea of Sorrow. The mind that is attached to words and concepts.

San (Jap). A suffix of respect like Mr., Mrs., or Miss.

sangha (Skt). The Buddhist community. Actually, all sentient beings.

śarīra (Skt). A bright mineral matter said to be found in the ashes after the body of a holy person is cremated.

satori (Skt). A glimpse of one's Buddha-nature which results in a fundamental revolution of the whole person.

Seizei (Jap) **Ch'ing-shui** (Ch) (ninth century). A Chinese disciple of Sozan.

sensei (Jap). Literally "teacher." Young zen priests usually use this title, reserving the title of *rōshi* for older, highly respected zen masters.

sesshin (Jap). Literally "searching the heart." Concentration of the mind. A period of intensive *zazen* practice usually lasting five to seven days, but sometimes lasting only one day. (See also *zazen*.)

Shakya (Skt) **Śākya** (P). The name of the Indian tribe in which Gautama Buddha was born. (See also Shakyamuni, Buddha, and Gautama Buddha.)

Shakyamuni (Skt) **Śākyamuni** (P). The silent sage *(muni)* of the Shakya tribe. A title which refers to Gautama Buddha. (See also Buddha, Gautama Buddha, and Shakya.)

shikan-taza (Jap) **chih-kuan ta-tsuo** (Ch). Just sitting. Themeless meditation. *Shikan* means "to give up illusions and attain enlightenment." *Taza* means "to sit wholeheartedly with the whole body and mind."

Shin (Jap). The Pure Land school of Buddhism. Sometimes known as Jōdo-shin or Jōdo-shinshu. This school relies on faith in the vows of Amida Buddha. (See also Amida Buddha, Jōdo, and Shinran.)

Shinran (Gutoku Shinran) (1173–1262). Founder of the Shin School of Buddhism. (See also Shin.)

Siddhartha (Skt). The given name of Gautama Buddha. It means "the successful one." (See also Buddha and Gautama Buddha.)

Snyder, Gary. An American zen poet. Winner in 1975 of the Pulitzer prize for poetry. Now living with his wife and two children in a cabin in the foothills of the Sierras near North San Juan, California.

Sokoji (Jap). The temple of the Japanese-American Zen Buddhist congregation in San Francisco which invited Suzuki Rōshi to America to become its priest. The temple was shared for many years with Suzuki Rōshi's American Zen Center students. (See also Suzuki Rōshi and Zen Center.)

Sōtō (Jap) **Ts'ao-tung** (Ch). A zen school stressing *shikan-taza* and everyday practice. According to this school, enlightenment and *zazen* are not different. (See also *shikan-taza*.)

Sozan (Jap) **T'sao-shan** (Ch). A famous Chinese zen master of the Sōtō school.

stupa (Skt). A dome-shaped monument marking a Buddhist sacred spot or sacred relics.

śūnyatā (Skt) **kū** (Jap). Emptiness. Void. A development of *anitya* (transience). *Śūnyatā* doesn't mean that everything is nonexistent. The void is full of concrete realities which interpenetrate each other, do not obstruct each other, but at the same time keep their individuality while continuing to change from moment to moment.

sūtra (Skt) **sutta** (P) **kyō** (Jap). Literally "a thread" on which the teachings were strung. A Buddhist scripture. From the mouth of the Buddha. A sermon, or seminar, of Gautama Buddha.

Sūtra of Hui-nêng (*Platform Sūtra on the Treasury of the Law*). The collection of sermons and sayings of the Sixth Chinese Zen Patriarch. The only Chinese work accorded the honored title of *sūtra*. (See also *sūtra* and Hui-nêng.)

Suzuki Rōshi (Shunryu Suzuki Rōshi). (1904–1971). Founder of Zen Center of San Francisco and Zenshinji Monastery in Tassajara, California, as well as several other smaller zen groups around the United States. Suzuki Rōshi was head of a large Zen Buddhist Temple complex in Japan but after he came to America in 1959 he decided to devote the rest of his life to teaching zen to Americans. When he resigned his position in his Japanese temple, his oldest son, who was also a zen priest, took his place. Although Suzuki Rōshi spent only twelve years in the United States, he attracted an unusually large number of strong zen students. He left an imprint of Bodhidharma upon the American zen environment. Marian Mountain became his student February 25, 1965. Her last visit with her zen master was at Tassajara, a few months before he passed away (December 1971). (See also Zen Center, Zenshinji, and Tassajara.)

tangaryo (Jap). A period of three to seven days of meditation in the vestibule of a temple or monastery by monks or zen students which demonstrates their sincerity and determination to be admitted to the monastic community. It is a formalization of the ancient custom of not admitting zen monks immediately to Buddhist temples, but making them wait outside the temple gates.

tantra (Skt). A scripture of an Indian school of mysticism which features esoteric or secret meditations. An important part of Tibetan Buddhism.

tao (Ch). Literally "the way," or "the path." A principle. A doctrine. The law, truth, or order of the universe. A way of life. A school of philosophy believed to have originated with the Chinese sage, Lao-tzu. (See also Lao-tzu.)

Tao-shêng (Ch) **Dōshō** (Jap) (Died 434). A Chinese Buddhist philosopher considered heretical during his lifetime for his position on the universal ecology of Buddha-nature. Later, when the complete *Nirvana Sūtra* was translated into Chinese, it was found that Tao-shêng's intuition was supported by Buddha.

Tassajara. The name of a valley in the Los Padres National Forest about forty miles from Carmel Valley, California. Site of mineral hot springs. Originally an Indian summer campsite. For one hundred years the location of the Tassajara Springs Resort. It was purchased by Zen Center of San Francisco in 1966 for a Zen Monastery (Zenshinji). During the summer guest season, zen students integrate zen practice with their work of running the resort. (See also Zenshinji.)

tatami (Jap). Rush mat. Traditional Japanese floor covering used in Japanese meditation halls.

Tatsugami Rōshi (Ryōsen Tatsugami Rōshi) (died 1979). A famous and respected contemporary zen master who served twelve years as head training master at Eiheiji Monastery in Japan. He was invited to come to California as a visiting abbot for two training periods at Zenshinji Monastery in 1970. At this time he accepted Marian Mountain as his disciple. (See also Zenshinji.)

taza-hara (Jap). "To sit in the posture of *zazen* in the center of existence." Two Japanese words combined in a new way by the author to emphasize a point about the zen environment.

Tenko San (Tenko Nishida) (1872–1968). A Japanese sage who founded the Ittoen way of life based on poverty, homelessness, and selfless service. (See also Ittoen.)

Three Worlds. The past, the present, and the future.

topsy-turvy views *viparyasa* (Skt) **tendō** (Jap). Sometimes called "perverted views." They are errors, or mistakes in thinking, or truth viewed in the wrong way. The four topsy-turvy views of Buddhism are the attachment to permanence, comfort, self, and sensual pleasure. In Zen Buddhism all forms of discrimination are considered topsy-turvy thinking.

Tosui (died 1683). A famous Sōtō Japanese zen master with many followers who gave up his respectable life to go and live with some beggars under a bridge in Kyoto.

Ummon (Jap) **Yün-mên** (Ch). Founder of a zen school in the Tang dynasty in China.

unsui (Jap). A zen trainee who leaves the monastery to seek the Buddha's way. Literally "cloud-water." (See also *gyōun-ryūsui*.)

Vimalakirti (Skt). The hero of the *Vimalakirti Sūtra* who was a wise lay Buddhist nobleman who had something to teach Buddha's great disciples.

wabi (Jap). Material and spiritual poverty. An unfashionable life. Solitariness. Simplicity.

wooden Buddha. When Tanka, a great zen master, was reprimanded for burning a wooden Buddha to warm himself, he denied he was being sacrilegious because he could find no *śarīra* in the ashes. (See *śarīra*.)

Wu-tzu Fa-yen (Ch) **Goso Hōyen** (Jap) (Died 1104). A famous Chinese zen master of the Sung dynasty.

yoga (Skt). Literally "to yoke," or "union." Union of *ātman* with *Brahman*, or soul with God. A way of life. A series of practices, including physical postures, which produce a state of tranquillity. (See also *ātman* and *Brahman*.)

zabuton (Jap.) A square, flat cushion used in meditation.

zafu (Jap). A fat round cushion used to sit on during *zazen*.

zazen (Jap). Sitting meditation. To meditate in the lotus posture. In the Sōtō school of Zen Buddhism, *zazen* is not considered a means to enlighten oneself; it is considered enlightenment itself. (See also lotus posture and Sōtō.)

zen (Jap) **ch'an** (Ch). Sitting meditation. A way of life. The human expression of universal truth.

Zen Buddhism (Jap). One of the schools of Buddhism. It features meditation and sudden enlightenment.

Zen Center (of San Francisco). An incorporation formed by a group of American students of Suzuki Rōshi in San Francisco in 1962. It has its headquarters at 300 Page St., San Francisco, California. (See also Suzuki Rōshi and Zentatsu Baker Rōshi.)

zen environment. Although this is a phrase created by the author to suggest the whole environment—inner as well as outer, spiritual as well as physical—the phrase can be used as a synonym for *nirvāna*, or *apratisthā*. The phrase is also related to the Sanskrit word *gocara* (kyō-gai in Jap), which means "the realm or environment to which one's power extends." Our sphere of influence may seem limited, but zen meditation helps us realize how our actions affect, and are affected by, an unlimited sphere.

zendō (Jap). *Zazen* hall. A room especially designed for zen meditation. (See also *zazen*.)

Zentatsu Baker Rōshi (Richard Baker Rōshi). Successor of Suzuki Rōshi. Abbot of Zen Center of San Francisco and Tassajara Monastery (Zenshinji) near Carmel Valley. (See also Zen Center and Suzuki Rōshi.)

Zenshinji (Jap). Zen Heart-Mind Temple. The zen monastery founded by Shunryu Suzuki Rōshi at Tassajara, California. (See also Suzuki Rōshi and Tassajara.)

Notes

For permission to use copyrighted material, grateful acknowledgement is extended to the following authors and publishers:

Dedication page: The quotation on *karma* is from the Japanese *Noh* play *Yama Uba (Yamamba)* or *Old Woman of the Mountains* and is translated by D. T. Suzuki in *Zen and Japanese Culture*, Bollingen Series LXIV (Princeton, N.J.: Princeton University Press, 1959), p. 426.

Introduction: The story of Joshu and Nansen is from the book *Eihei-Shingi (Regulations for the Monastic Life)* by Dogen Zenji, and is translated by Dainin Katagiri Roshi.

Page 8 D. T. Suzuki, op. cit., p. 172.

Page 8 Ibid., p. 125.

Page 8 I have not been able to locate the source of this translation.

Page 26 Marshall McLuhan. *Understanding Media: The Extensions of Man* (New York: McGraw-Hill Paperbacks, 1964), p. 25.

Page 30 Carlos Castaneda, *Journey to Ixtlan: Lessons of Don Juan* (New York: Touchstone/Simon & Schuster, 1972). Since Dr. Castaneda does not give permission to use direct quotations from his books, I have had to paraphrase his words. I urge anyone who has not read the original to do so. Much of the spirit of Don Juan's teachings are lost in my secondhand report.

Page 31 Gary Snyder, *Riprap and Cold Mountain Poems* (Bolinas, Cal.: Four Seasons Foundation, 1966), pp. 43 & 47.

Page 31 Ibid., p. 39.

Page 38 D. T. Suzuki, *Essays in Zen Buddhism, First Series* (New York: Grove Press, 1961), p. 40.

Page 53 Shunryu Suzuki, *Zen Mind, Beginner's Mind* (New York and Tokyo: Weatherhill, 1970), pp. 111–112.

Page 61 I read about the tick in John Bleibtreau's book *The Parable of the Beast.*

Page 76 D. T. Suzuki, *Essays;* op. cit., p. 45.

Page 79 Shunryu Suzuki, op. cit., p. 25.

Page 84 Ibid., p. 26.

Page 84 Ibid., p. 26.

Page 85 Ibid., p. 26.

Page 98 Ibid., p. 116.

Page 101 Ibid., p. 45.

Page 110 Carl Seelig, *Albert Einstein* (Zurich: Europa Verlag, 1954).

Pages 110–111 John Blofeld, *The Zen Teachings of Huang Po* (New York: Grove Press, 1958), p. 63.

Page 112 Yūhō Yokoi, *Zen Master Dōgen* (New York and Tokyo: Weatherhill, 1976), p. 51.

Page 115 John Blofeld, op. cit., p. 71.

Page 118 Shunryu Suzuki, op. cit., p. 58.

Page 120 From the zen story "The Taste of Banzo's Sword," in Paul Reps, *Zen Flesh, Zen Bones* (Garden City, N.Y.: Anchor Books/Doubleday, 1957), p. 74–75.

Pages 127–128 Carlos Castaneda, op. cit.

Pages 128–129 Edward Conze, *Buddhist Thought in India* (Ann Arbor: University of Michigan Press, 1962), p. 274.

Page 141 *Wind Bell*, Vol. XII (1973), p. 20. Published by Zen Center, 300 Page St., San Francisco, Cal.

Page 141 From the zen story "Fire-Poker Zen," in Paul Reps, op. cit., p. 76.

Page 147 *Wind Bell*, Vol XIV No. 1. (Summer 1975), p. 16.

Page 153 From *The Sayings of Goso Hoyen,* translated by D. T. Suzuki in *Zen and Japanese Culture,* op. cit., p. 10.

Page 154 Ibid., pp. 9–10.

Page 154 From the zen story "Non-Attachment," in Paul Reps, op. cit., pp. 80–81.

Pages 154–155 From the zen story "Zen in a Beggar's Life," in Paul Reps, op. cit., p. 40.

Page 155 From the zen story "Tosui's Vinegar," in Paul Reps, op. cit., p. 81.

Page 160 From the zen story "Seizei Alone and Poor," in Paul Reps, op. cit., p. 98.

Page 161 From the zen story "The Moon Cannot be Stolen," in Paul Reps, op. cit., p. 12.

Page 162 Ittoen Tenko-San; *A New Road to Ancient Truth,* Makoto Ohashi and Marie Byles (New York: Horizon Press, 1969).

Page 168 Thich Nhat Hahn, *Zen Keys* (Garden City, N.Y.: Anchor Books/Doubleday, 1973), p. 138.

Page 172 Ittoen Tenko-San, op. cit., p. 62.

Page 173 Dōgen Zenji, "Genjo-kōan," translated by Rev. Rōshi Jiyu-Kennett in *Zen is Eternal Life* (Dharma Publishing, 1976), p. 174.

Page 174 From the zen story "The Stingy Artist," in Paul Reps, op. cit., pp. 43–44.

Page 175 Lama Anagarika Govinda, "Siddas and Zen Buddhism," in *Wind Bell,* Vol. IX, No. 1 (Winter 1970), p. 42.

Pages 175–176 Ittoen Tenko-San, op. cit., p. 73.

Page 179 Carlos Castaneda, op. cit.

Page 193 Yūhō Yokoi, op. cit., p. 95.

Page 194 Shunryu Suzuki, op. cit., p. 133.

Page 197 *Wind Bell,* Vol. XIII, Nos. 1–2. (1974), p. 28.

Pages 198–199 Shunryu Suzuki, op. cit., p. 138.

Index

ABOUT THE AUTHOR

MARIAN MOUNTAIN lives in the Ventana
Wilderness of Big Sur, California, with
her husband, Jack. *The Zen Environment* is
her first book.

☐ **SPACE-TIME AND BEYOND** by Bob Toben and
<u>Fred Alan Wolf</u> (13129-X * $2.95)
Here is the classic work on the new physics and expanded
consciousness now in a new, completely updated edition.
Through simple, illuminating drawings and commentary,
the authors translate the most difficult concepts of modern
physics and the "unexplainable" wonders of paranormal
psychology into clear, comprehensible thoughts.